Sylvain Lecombre

ZADKINE MUSEUM GUIDE

PARIS musées

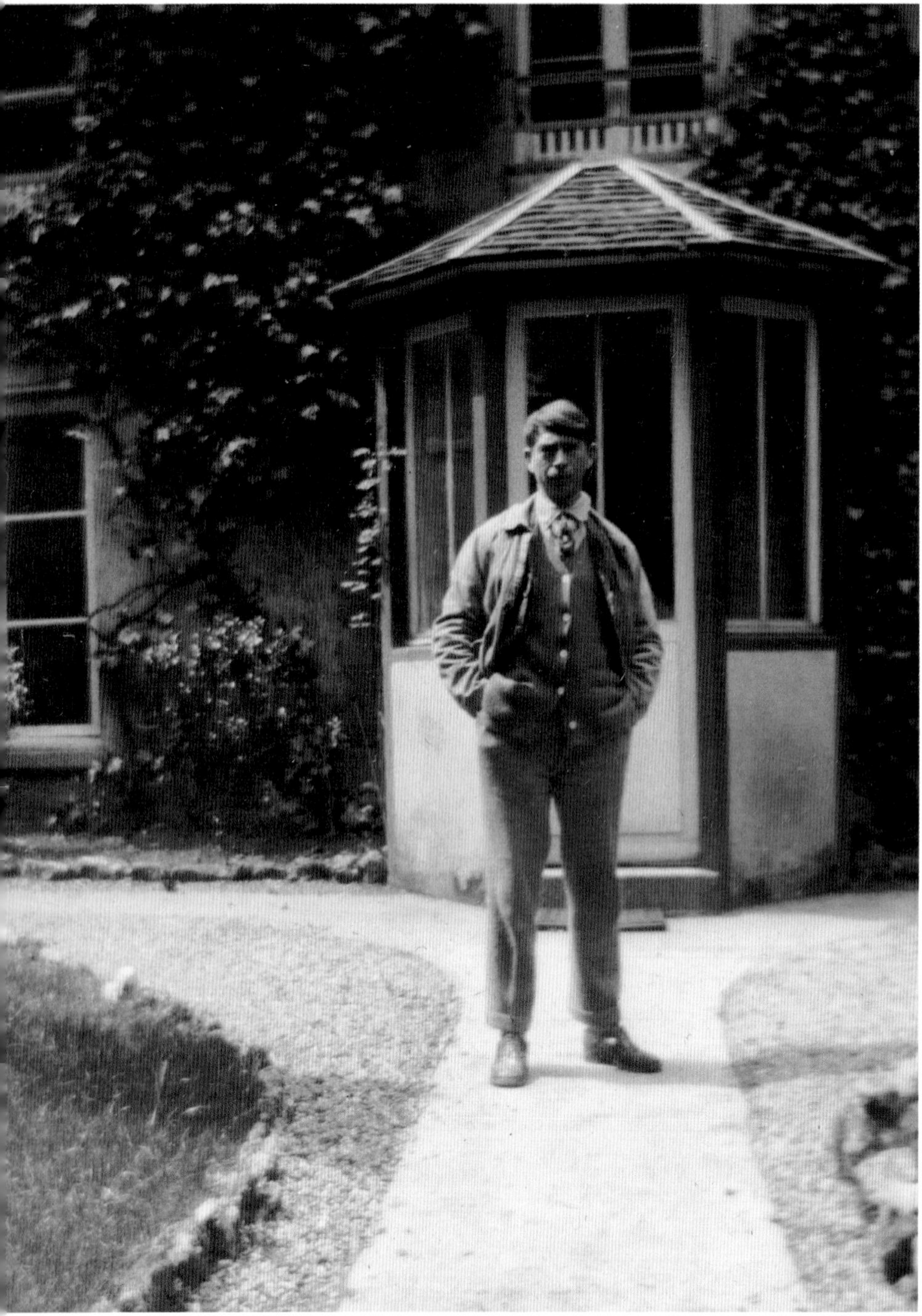

Ossip Zadkine outside his house, Rue d'Assas, Paris, c. 1930

Contents

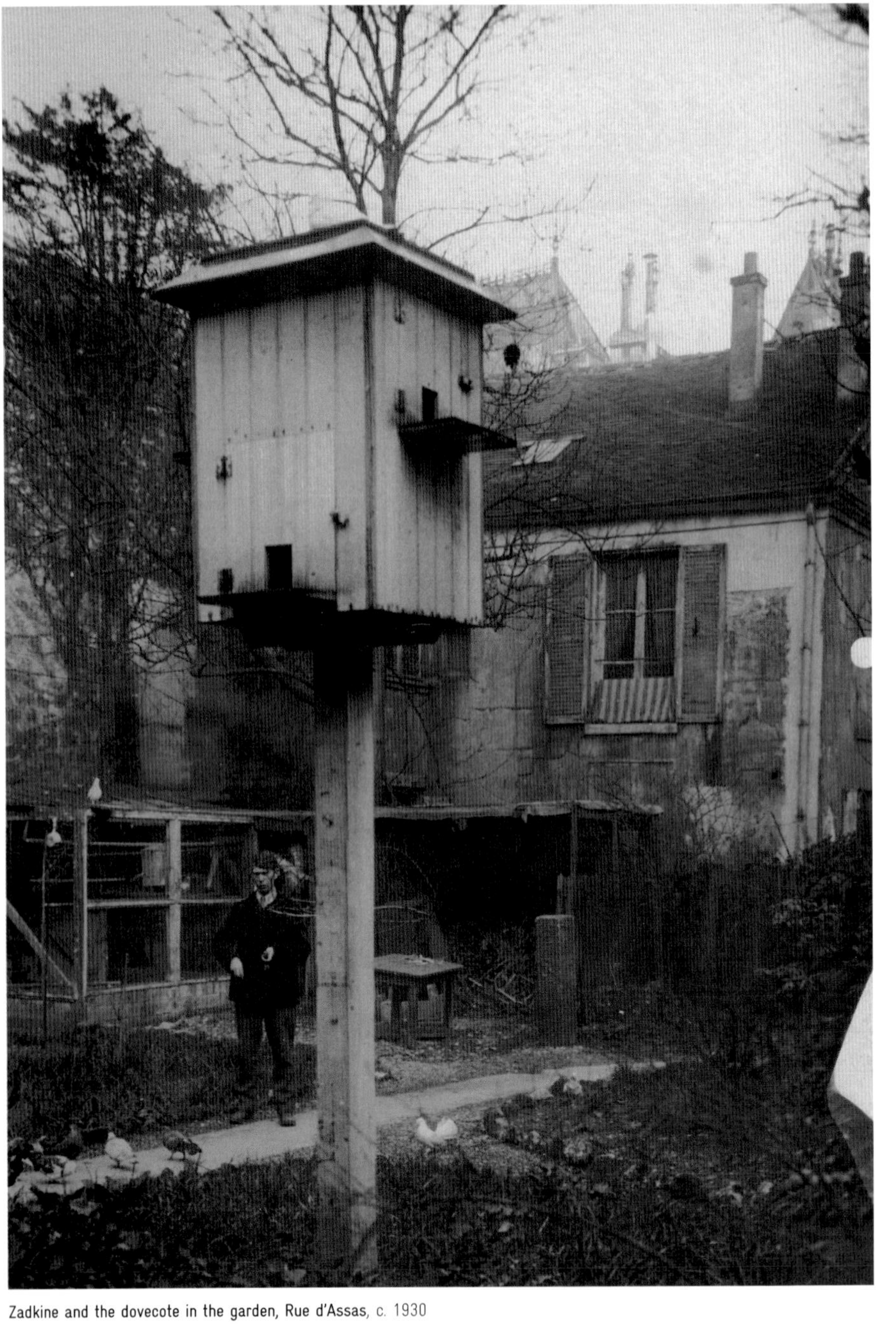

Zadkine and the dovecote in the garden, Rue d'Assas, c. 1930

Foreword

Having just bought the house in Rue Assas that is now his personal Paris museum, on 11 April 1928 Ossip Zadkine wrote to his art critic friend André de Ridder, "It's as if I've been transplanted and I still don't know if it's real! Come and see my 'Assas folly' and you'll understand how a man's life can be changed by a dovecote and a tree."
In his book *Zadkine* (Gallimard, 1930), Pierre Humbourg describes the artist's living and working environment: "The setting is an oasis in the heart of Paris: a garden that is 'trim, ridiculous and charming', an aviary with a noisy chaffinch, a dovecote, dying trees, and bits of statues growing up out of the rich soil. The studio is delightfully disorderly and there, in amongst all his works, is Zadkine, smiling."

Today the place has lost none of its charm and intimate feel, even if changes have been needed to make allowance for visitors and a presentation of the development of the Zadkine oeuvre.
The museum was officially founded by the City of Paris in April 1982. We owe its existence to the determination of the sculptor's wife, the painter Valentine Prax (1897–1981), who made it a prerequisite for an initial donation and for making the City of Paris her sole legatee.
The collection bequeathed by Valentine Prax comprises over 380 sculptures and more than 350 works on paper.
The income from her legacy and from sales of the bronze copies the City has the right to produce in stipulated quantities enables the museum to keep adding to its collection. Since it opened seventeen more sculptures have been acquired, together with eighteen works on paper – mainly gouaches and watercolours from the twenties and thirties, periods not represented in the original legacy.

In addition the museum's archives, which are available for consultation by appointment, are home to other material – letters, manuscripts, photographs, catalogues – bearing on Zadkine's career and his relationships with dealers, critics, collectors, institutions, pupils, artists and writers.

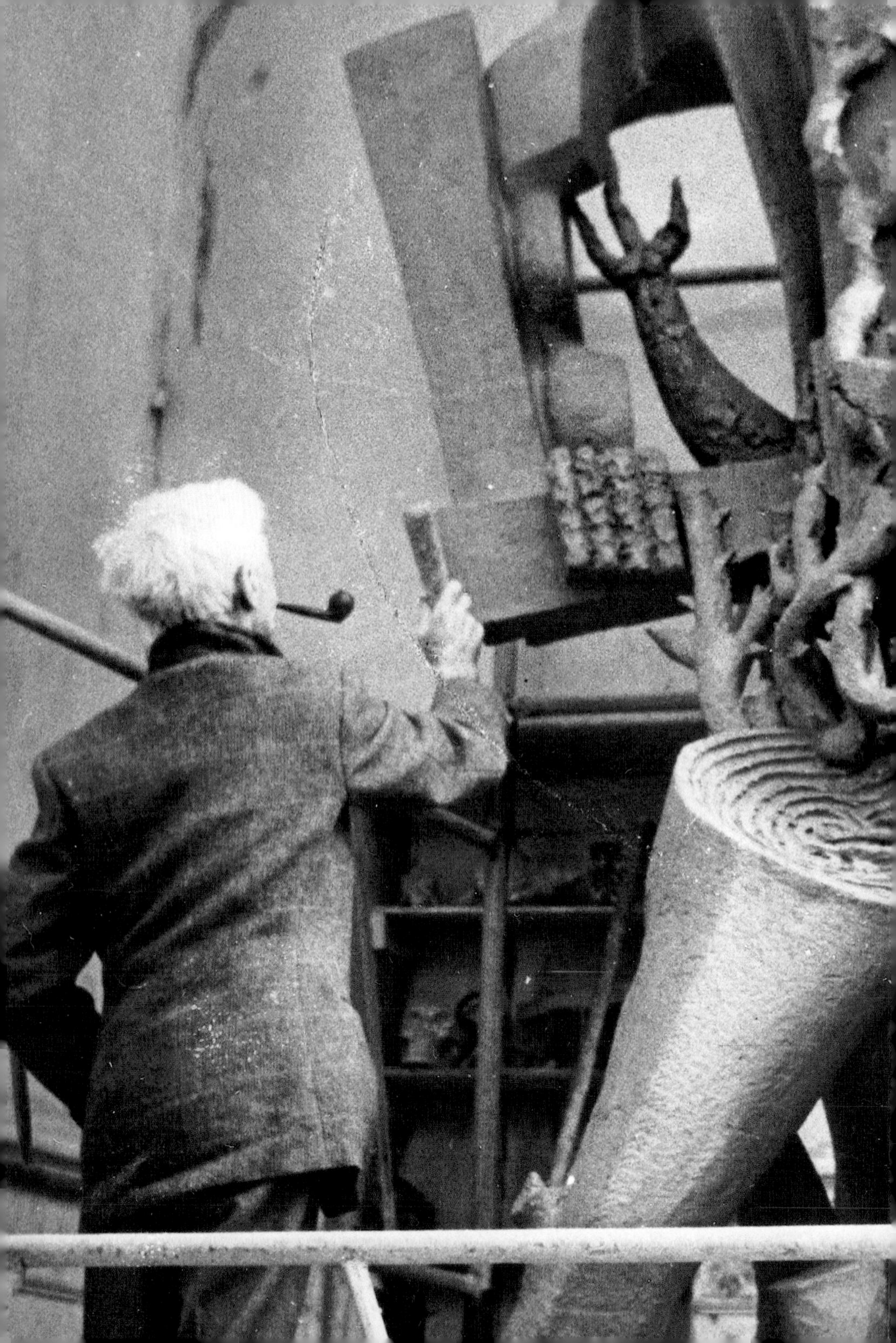

Zadkine: the Life

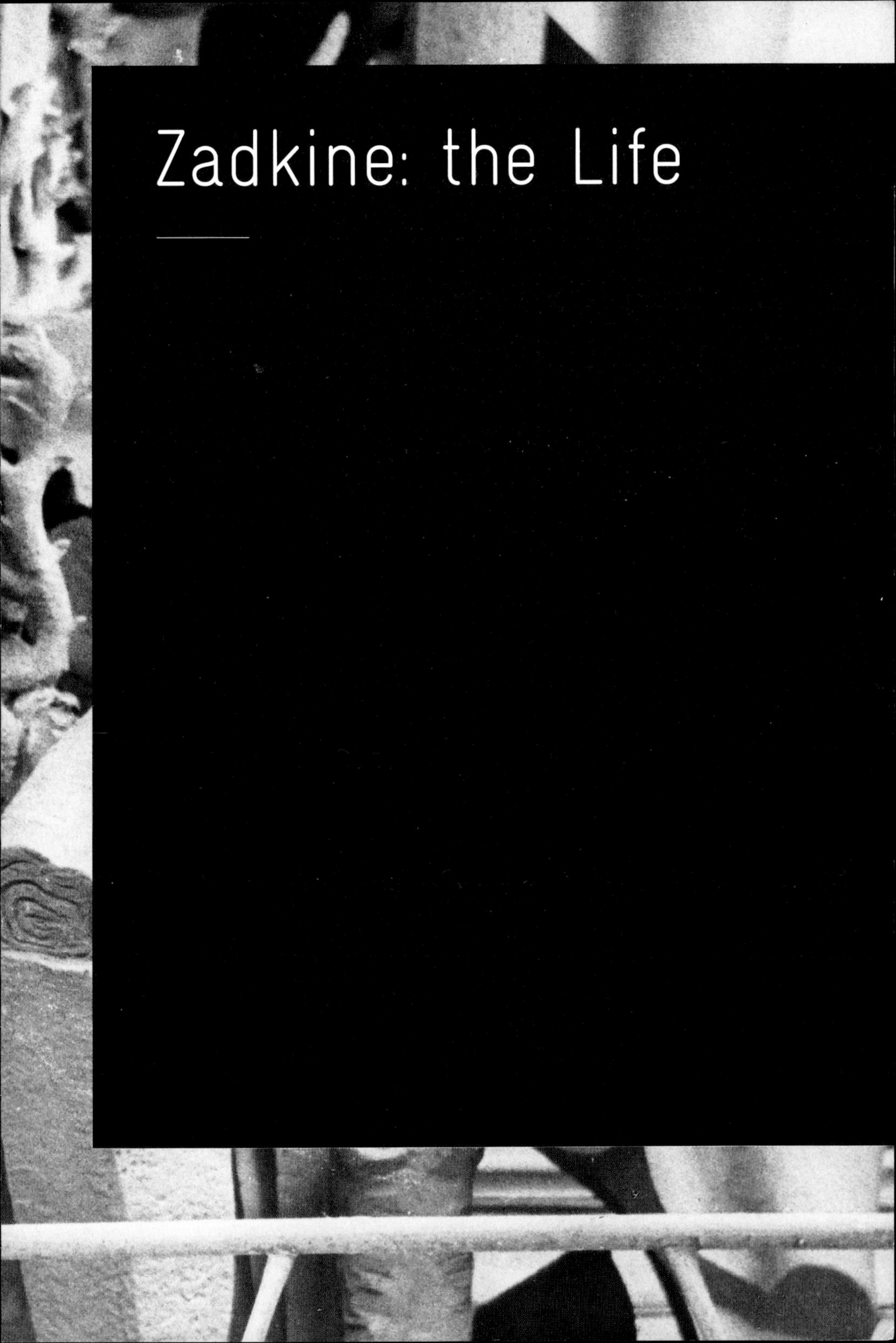

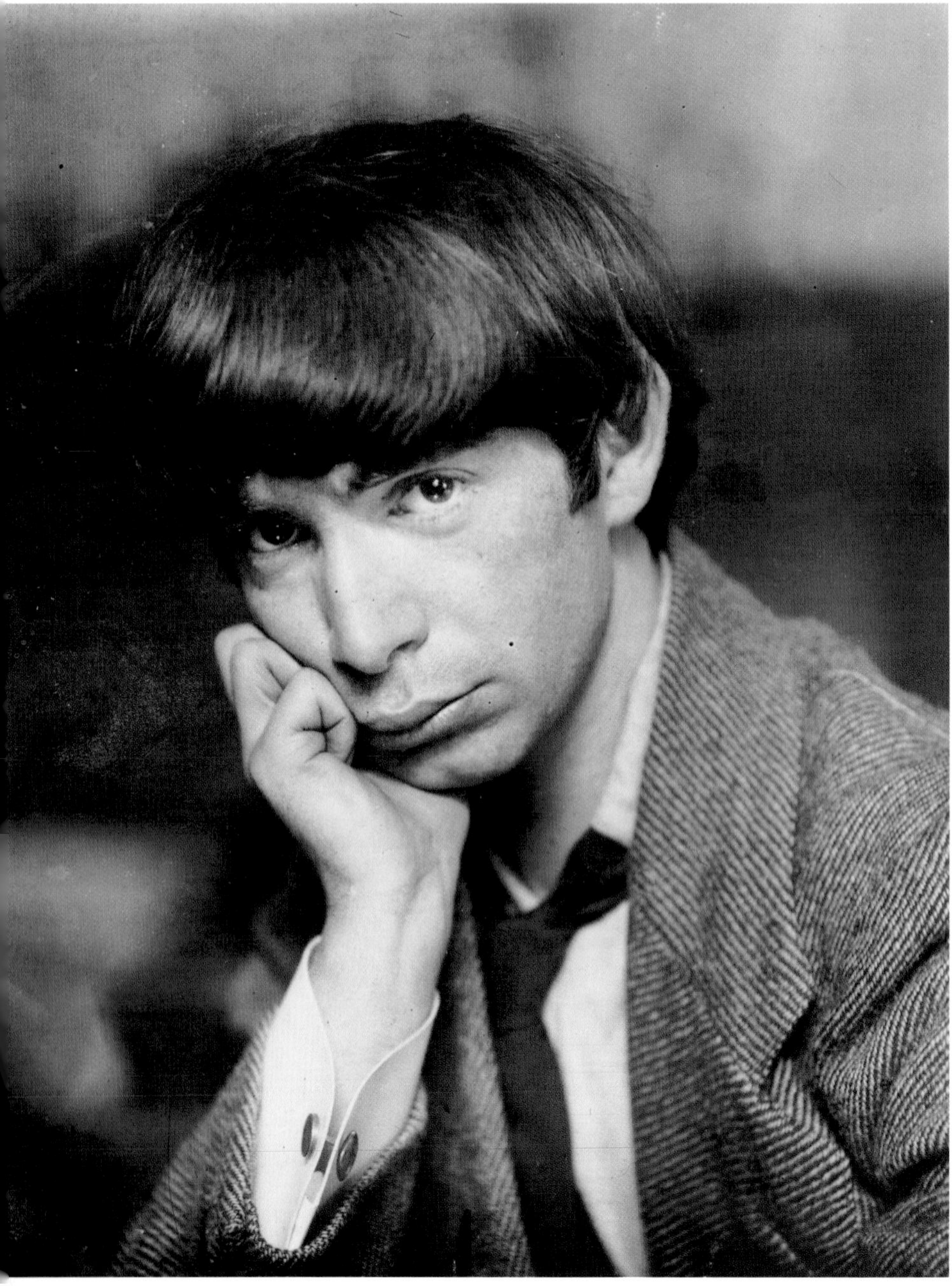

Ossip Zadkine, c. 1914

1890-1917

Ossip Zadkine is born on 4 July 1890 in Vitebsk, in today's Belarus. His mother's Scottish ancestors had moved to Russia in the 17th century and his father, of Jewish descent, has converted to the Orthodox faith in order to marry her.
Zadkine spends his childhood in Smolensk, in Russia, where his father teaches classics at the seminary and his uncle builds wooden ships that ply the Dnieper and Dvina rivers. He grows up in the setting of forests, rivers and wooden houses that will mark him for life. His artistic inclinations appear very early and he makes his first sculptures while still a child.
At the age of fifteen he is sent by his parents to live with an uncle in Sunderland, in the north of England. Alert to the boy's talents, the uncle enrols him at the local art school.

Zadkine later moves in with a friend in London to pursue his art training, but spends most of his time visiting museums. He also becomes an apprentice furniture-maker and learns ornamental sculpture, acquiring the technical skills which will stand him in such good stead in the carvings to come. He makes his first contacts with critics and artists, among them the sculptor Jacob Epstein.

Next stop Paris, where he arrives in 1910. He enrols at the Ecole des Beaux-Arts, but leaves after six months, dissatisfied with the academic approach that still prevails there. More instructive are his visits to the Louvre: "We used to discuss the sculptures we saw there," he writes in *Le Maillet et le Ciseau* (Hammer and Chisel), "and with the very limited French picked up from my reading I would discourse about Egyptian sculpture. At that time we made really dramatic discoveries. One morning one of us showed the others a photo of a Roman head. The formal simplicity and size, and the emotion emanating from the eyes left us disgusted with the pale imitations we were modelling at art school. Obscurely we felt that it was inside this kind of ancient work that the key to the world of sculpture was hidden."

Like such other sculptors of his generation as Amedeo Modigliani, Alexander Archipenko, Henri Gaudier-Brzeska – and Constantin Brancusi before them – Zadkine goes down the

Primitivist/Archaist trail blazed by Gauguin late in the 19th century. The profound change in modes of expression this calls for can only be achieved by a radical break: not only with the Academic tradition, but also with the oeuvre of Rodin, whose influence an entire generation is now trying to cut free of.
Zadkine first exhibits in 1911, showing six sculptures and a drawing at the Société Nationale des Beaux-Arts, then at the Salon des Indépendants.
He is now living in La Ruche (The Beehive), an artists' studio complex founded in 1902 by the sculptor Alfred Boucher, who has transplanted buildings from the 1900 Universal Exposition to Paris's Vaugirard neighbourhood. In 1912 Zadkine moves to 114 Rue de Vaugirard and then, in 1915, to 35 Rue Rousselet.

He further asserts his presence on the contemporary art scene with nine sculptures and three drawings at the Salon d'Automne in 1913, and with his first exhibitions abroad, in Berlin and Amsterdam, as well as in London, where sculptor Henri Gaudier-Brzeska writes about his work in the review *The Egoist*.

Zadkine is also part of the intellectual and artistic ferment that is beginning to bring Montparnasse an international reputation: receptions at the Boulevard Raspail residence of Baroness d'Oettingen, a backer of Guillaume Apollinaire's review *Les Soirées de Paris*; artists' get-togethers at the Russian Academy founded by Marie Vassilieff in Avenue du Maine; concerts, plays and exhibitions at the Lyre et Palette in Rue Huyghens, where he also exhibits in May 1917; and contributions to the reviews *Les Lettres Parisiennes*, *SIC* and *Montparnasse*. He also has his portrait drawn by Modigliani, his friend and already a local legend.

In response to the call from Blaise Cendrars and Ricciotto Canudo for artists to take part in the War, he signs up as a stretcher-bearer on 24 January 1916. Assigned to the French army's Russian Ambulance Corps, he is gassed on the Champagne front in November 1916 and put on indefinite leave in October 1917. During this period he produces a remarkable series of drawings and watercolours, most of them now in the Musée d'Histoire Contemporaine (BDIC) in Paris, together with a set of engravings published in 1918 as *Twenty Etchings Drawn and Engraved by Ossip Zadkine, soldier in the 1st Foreign Regiment of the French Army Russian Ambulance Corps*.

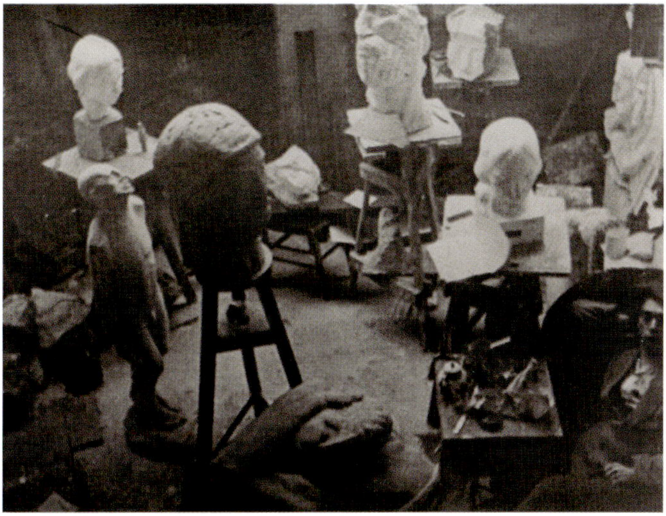

Zadkine in his La Ruche studio, 1912

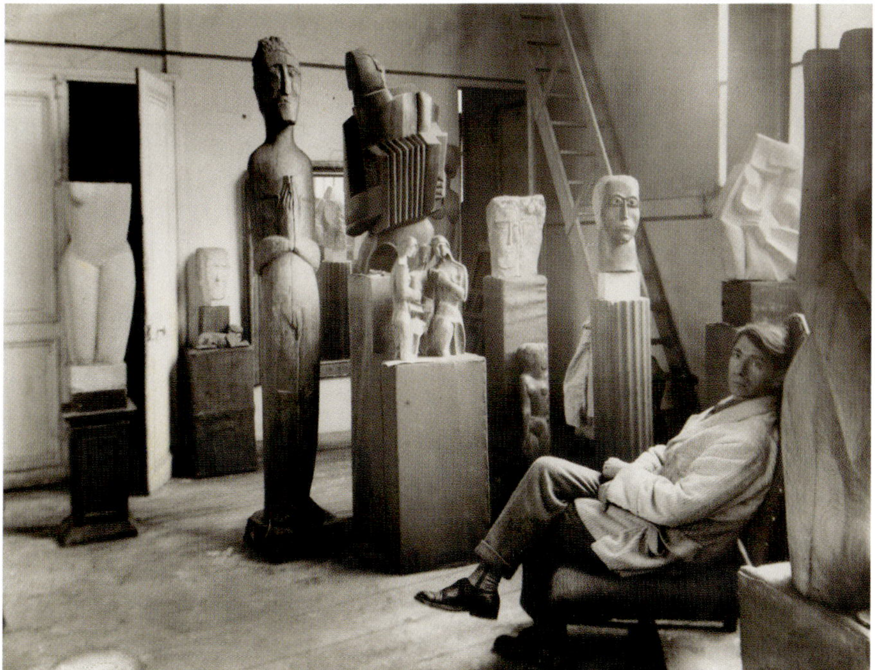

Zadkine in his Rue Rousselet studio, c. 1926

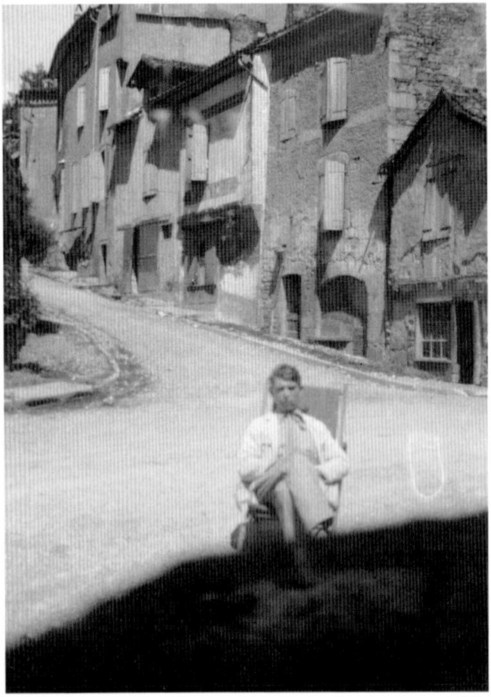

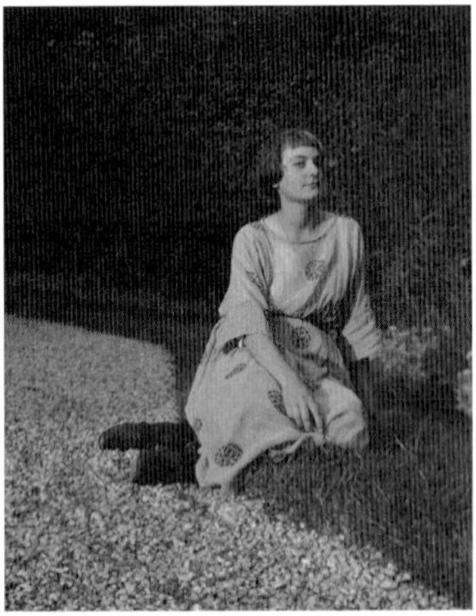

Zadkine in the street in Bruniquel, South-Western France, c. 1920

Valentine Prax (1897-1981), c. 1930

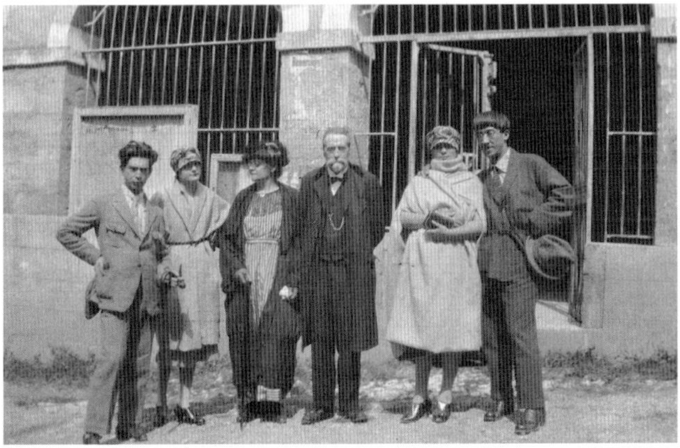

The wedding of Ossip Zadkine and Valentine Prax in Bruniquel, 1920. With them are the bride's parents, the Japanese painter Foujita and his wife Fernande Barrey

1918-1920

The discovery of the South of France – he is invited by his painter friend Henry Ramey to the village of Bruniquel, not far from Montauban – is a major event in Zadkine's life. There he embarks on a prolific output of gouaches and watercolours: landscapes, views of villages, and nudes in landscapes. He will remain very attached to the region, buying a house first in Caylus, in the Tarn-et-Garonne département, and then in Les Arques, in the Lot département, in 1934.
In 1918 he exhibits at the Galerie Chappe-Lautier in Toulouse: four "direct" sculptures, three terracotta pieces, fifty-seven works on paper and the war etchings. The introductory text for the exhibition is by the painter Roger Bissière.
At the 1919 Salon d'Automne he shows four remarkable wood sculptures: *The Grape Harvest* (Musée Zadkine), *Job* (Antwerp, Musée des Beaux-Arts), *The Messenger* (Musée de Grenoble) and *Motherhood*.
The year 1920 is marked by two major events. He marries his Bruniquel neighbour, the young painter Valentine Prax, and organises his first solo exhibition in his studio: forty-nine sculptures in wood, stone and marble, thirty watercolours and thirty drawings. The catalogue preface is by art critic Georges Duthuit.
1920 also sees him make contact with the Antwerp review *Sélection*, edited by Paul-Gustave Van Hecke and André de Ridder. Later the Zadkine oeuvre will become much appreciated in Belgium – and even more so in Holland.

1921-1925

Introduced by critic Maurice Raynal to the artists associated with the Rome review *Valori Plastici*, Zadkine is the sole fully-fledged foreign member to show at the exhibition devoted to the group by the National Gallery in Berlin in April 1921; the other participants are sculptor Arturo Martini and painters Carlo Carrà, Giorgio De Chirico, Giorgio Morandi and Roberto Melli. The same year Maurice Raynal writes the first monograph on his work, published by *Valori Plastici* with twenty-nine reproductions.

In Paris Dr Girardin has just opened his La Licorne gallery and in 1921 Zadkine shows the handsome group of marble sculptures dating from 1918–20. Girardin will later leave his extensive collection to the City of Paris.

The same year sees the first acquisitions of Zadkine's work by a museum: Pierre Andry-Farcy, a curator receptive to the contemporary, buys *Tiger*, in gilt wood, and a marble *Head of a Girl* for the museum in Grenoble.

In the early twenties he begins to take a Cubist tack: at the Salon d'Automne in 1923 he shows *Woman with a Fan*, whose frankly geometrical lines are his clearest assertion of this adoption of the movement's rigorous principles. Nonetheless he produces few pieces in this spirit and will soon bring more fluidity and humanity to his work.
In addition, the seal is set on his reputation with a major exposition at the Galerie Barbazanges, one of Paris's most prestigious venues.

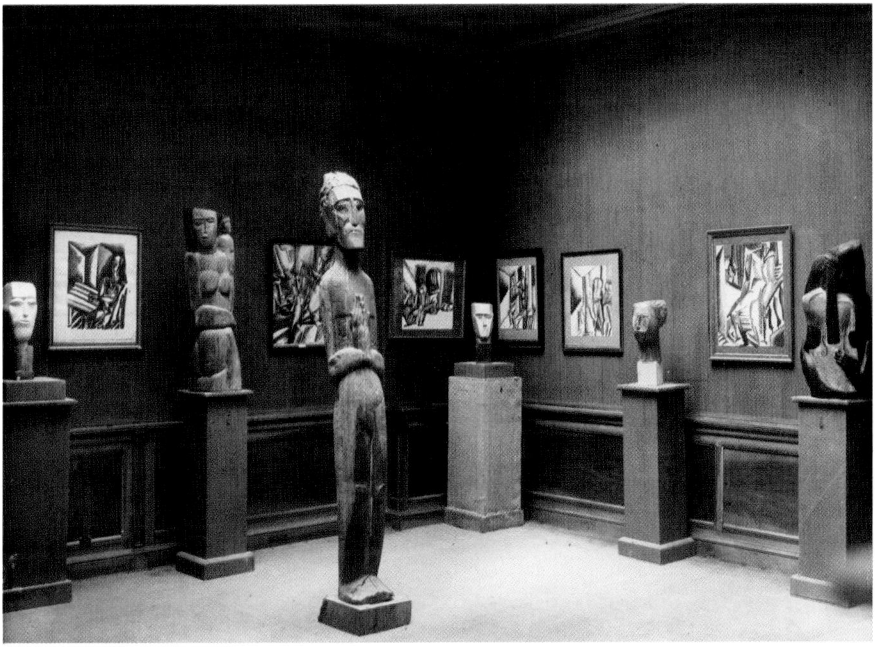

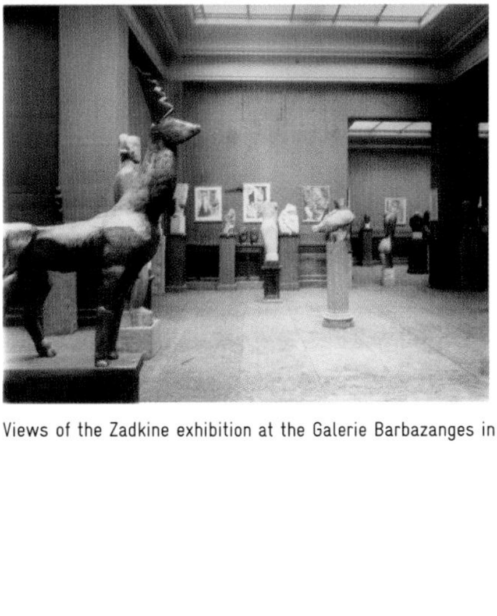

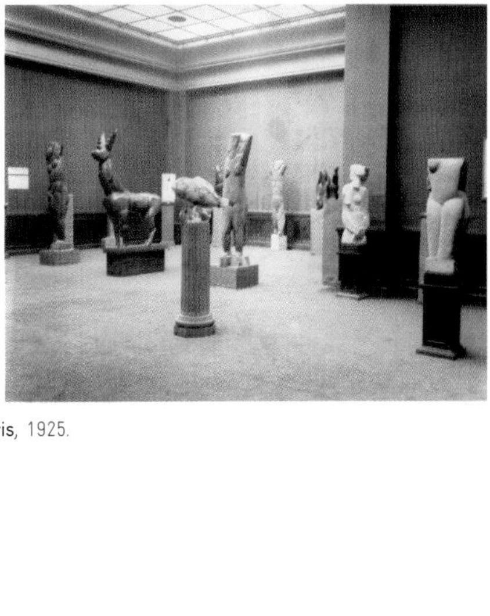

Views of the Zadkine exhibition at the Galerie Barbazanges in Paris, 1925.

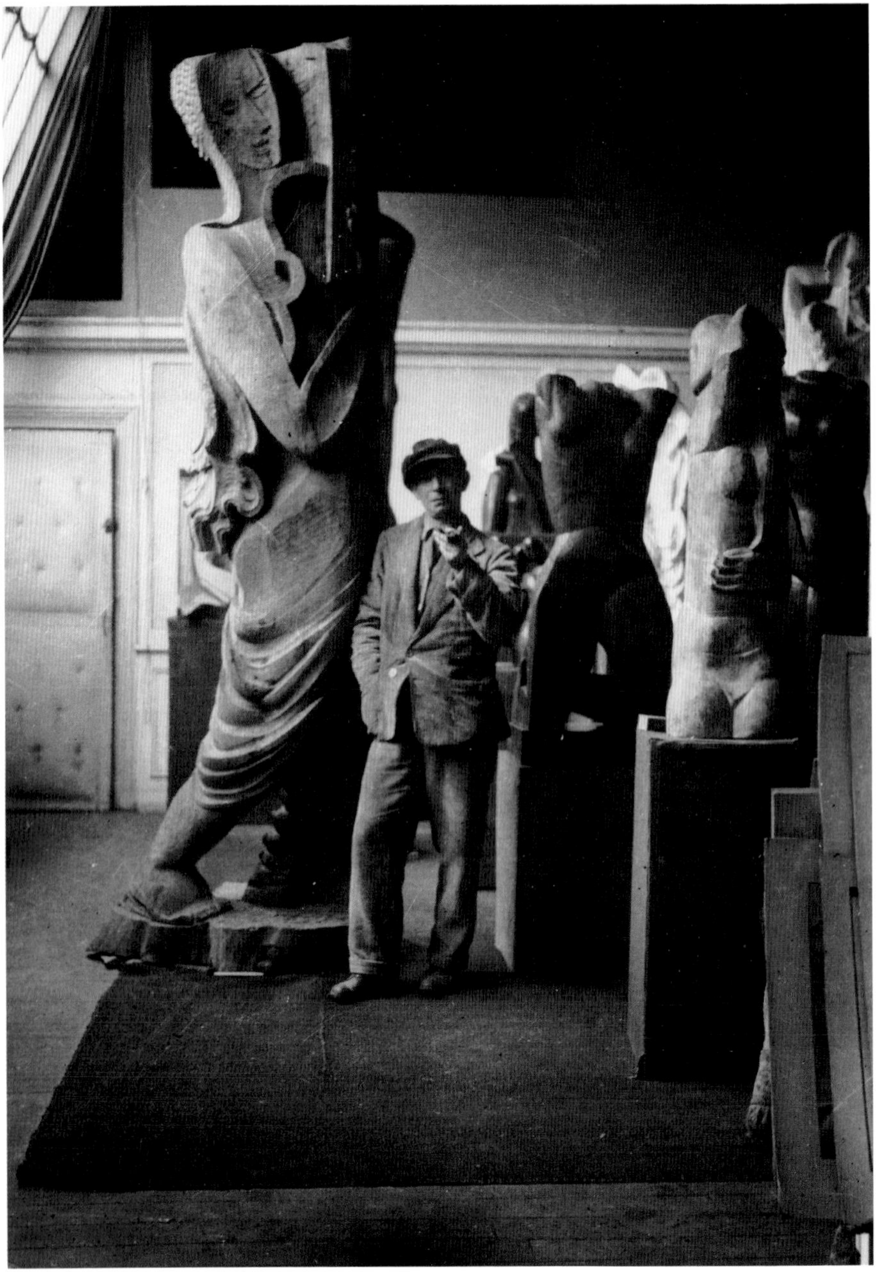

Zadkine in his Rue d'Assas studio with his wood sculpture *Orpheus*, 1930

1926-1941

Shown at the Salon des Tuileries in 1926, the bronzes *Pomona* and *The Three Graces* mark a turning point in an oeuvre hitherto almost exclusively devoted to direct carving.

The exhibition of his *Maenads* at the Salon d'Automne in 1929 is another significant advance: with it he definitively leaves Archaism behind, henceforth seeking inspiration in Greek sculpture and imbuing his works with the easy flow of classical drapery.
No longer massively hermetic blocks, his sculptures relate to the space around them in a more formally complex way, with convexity and concavity also increasingly important. Mythology, too, becomes a source of inspiration. These changes are eloquently illustrated by three crucial works from 1930: *Birth of Venus*, *Laocoon* and his first *Orpheus*, carved in wood.
In a return to his inspirational roots, he makes a trip to Greece in 1931.

In 1939 the roughs for monuments to Guillaume Apollinaire, Arthur Rimbaud, the Comte de Lautréamont and Alfred Jarry go on show at the Galerie Montaigne in Paris; these represent the groundwork for the lyrical proliferation that will characterise the sculpture of the fifties and sixties.
These years also see Zadkine's reputation consolidated by a number of solo exhibitions: in London, at the Arthur Tooth Gallery in 1928; in Room 13 of the Italian Pavilion at the 1932 Venice Biennale; and, for his first visit to the United Sates, at the Brummer Gallery in New York in 1937.

When World War Two breaks out his American friends advise him to leave Europe, and in December 1940 he unwillingly opts for exile. Obtaining his American visa in late May 1941, he sets sail from Lisbon on 20 June.

1941-1944

"My life in America was spent in a fog, in a kind of drying-up of my imagination," he writes in *Le Maillet et le Ciseau*. It must be said that only two memorable works date from this period, both of them reactions to historical circumstance: his *Phoenix* – the symbol of resurrection – and more notably *The Prisoner*, referred to in his diary as "that sinister hen coop". Likewise the vigorous series of drawings *The Labours of Hercules* (1943) echoes the dramatic confrontations of the time.

On arriving in the United States he begins teaching, at Black Mountain College in North Carolina and more especially at the Art Students League in New York. This is an activity he will carry on when he returns to Paris, mainly for the benefit of American students, in his Rue Notre-Dame-des-Champs studio ("The Ossip Zadkine Studio of Modern Sculpture and Drawing") and at the Académie de la Grande Chaumière.

Invited to take part in the "Artists in Exile" exhibition at the Pierre Matisse Gallery in New York in 1942, he finds himself in eminent company: Fernand Léger, Max Ernst, Marc Chagall, Piet Mondrian and others. He also has solo exhibitions at three important galleries: Wildenstein (1941), Curt Valentin (1943) and Bignou (1944).

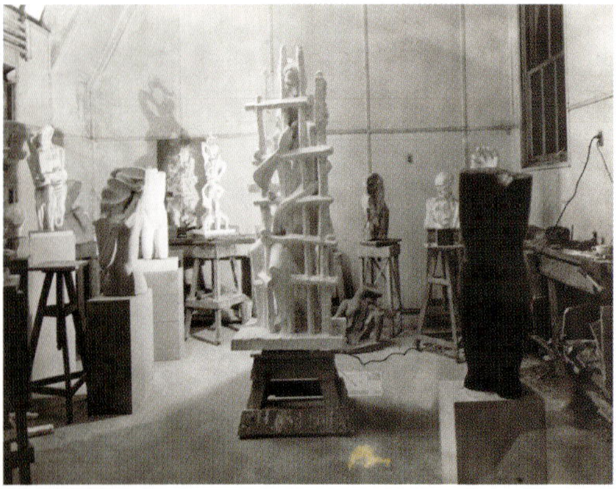

Zadkine's New York studio: in the centre, the plaster cast of *The Prisoner*, 1943

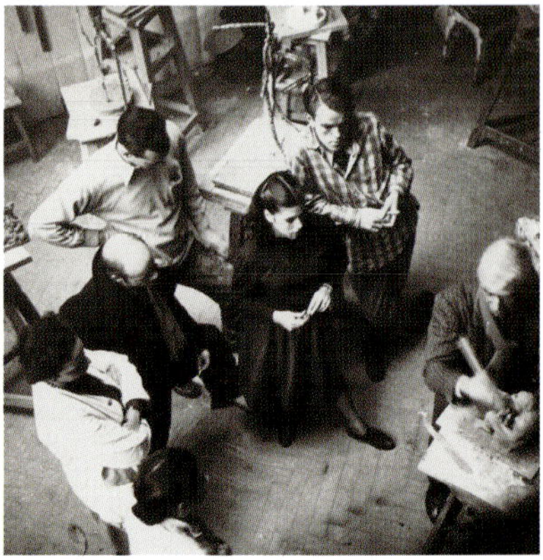

Zadkine with his pupils, c. 1960

1945-1958

Once back in France, he quickly finds an upsurge of creative energy.
"I remember that when I saw the 'ghosts' - my New York sculptures - I knew I had to make a change and start building afresh, putting America out of my mind. I began with a group of three figures whose lower part was like the aftermath of some disaster - shattered, chaotic, humiliated - with the top part holed but rebuilt. I was facing the human forest."

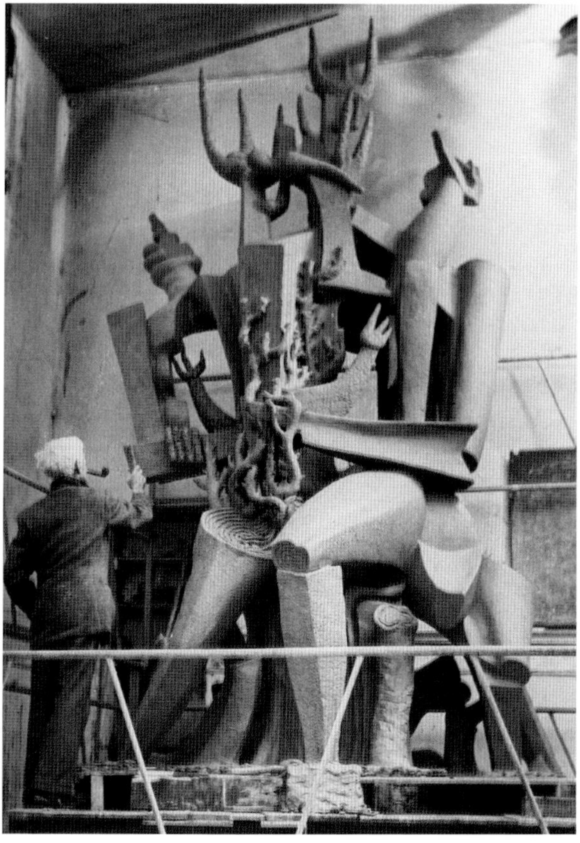

Zadkine inspecting *The Human Forest*, commissioned by the Van Leer Foundation in Jerusalem, 1960

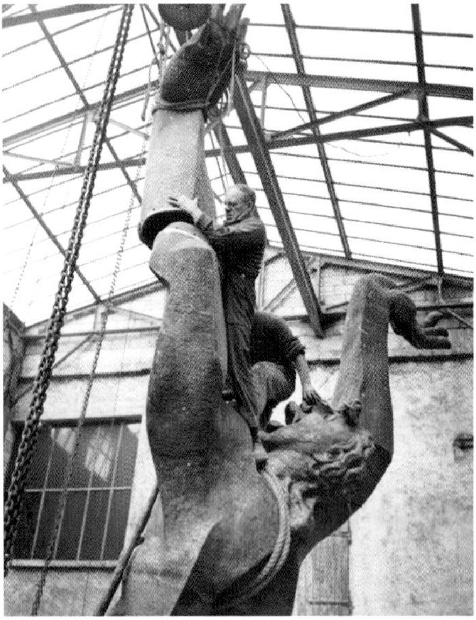

To a Destroyed City at the Susse foundry, 1951

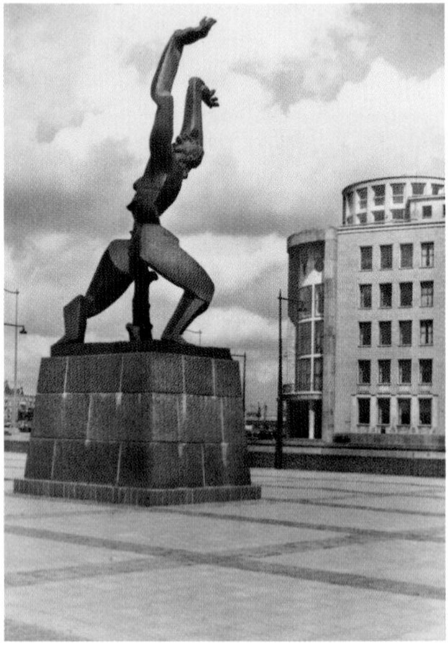

To a Destroyed City on Leuvehaven, Rotterdam

In the same spirit he makes *Birth of Forms* (1947) and in 1948 his first postwar *Orpheus*, very different in its spareness, vertical thrust and pathos from the 1930s version. Appalled by the devastation he sees in Le Havre and Rotterdam, in 1947 he shows in Berlin and Prague his preliminary version of *To a Destroyed City*. Dutch friends who want the project realised in Rotterdam as a symbol of their city's destruction and resurrection provide financial backing; in 1949 Rotterdam becomes the focus for the venture and in October 1950 *Time* magazine announces that Zadkine has been given the go-ahead for a sculpture with the same symbolic impact as Picasso's *Guernica*. The unveiling takes place on 24 April 1953 and the image of *To a Destroyed City* – its creator's most famous work – is seen around the world.

The resultant international recognition is confirmed by Zadkine's winning of the Sculpture Prize at the 1950 Venice Biennale.

Still in 1950, he takes part in the exhibition "Sacred Art: French Works of the 19th and 20th Centuries" at the Musée National d'Art Moderne. Sacred art is undergoing a dazzling revival, with results to be seen in works by artists as famous as Fernand Léger and Marc Chagall. Zadkine had carved a large Christ in 1938–40 and a second one, dating from 1951, is acquired in 1952 for the church in Caylus. In 1955–57 he sculpts a *Pietà* now in the village church in Les Arques.

1956 brings a commission for a monument to Vincent Van Gogh, unveiled in Auvers-sur-Oise in 1961. This tribute to a painter Zadkine loved for his lyricism and expression of emotion is followed by others: for the Dutch town of Zundert, where the Van Gogh brothers were born; Saint-Rémy-de-Provence in France; and Wasmes in Belgium.
During this period major Zadkine exhibitions are held: at the Antwerp Fine Arts Association and the Palais des Beaux-Arts in Brussels in 1948; the Musée National d'Art Moderne in Paris and the Boymans Museum, Rotterdam, in 1949; and the Maison de la Pensée Française in Paris in 1958.
In 1954 comes his first solo exhibition in Japan, at the Fujikawa Gallery.

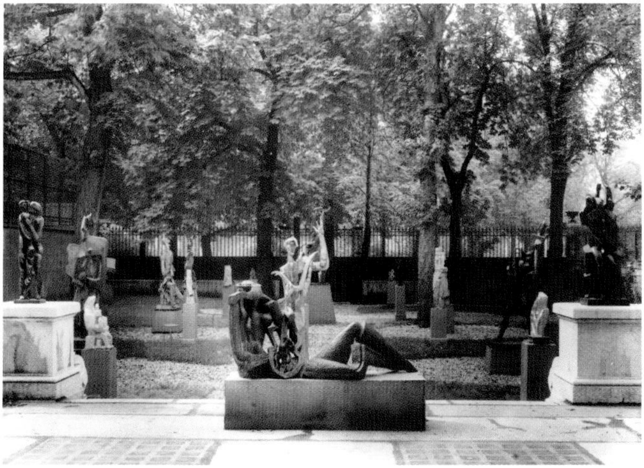

Sculptures by Zadkine in the garden of the Maison de la Pensée Française, Paris, 1958

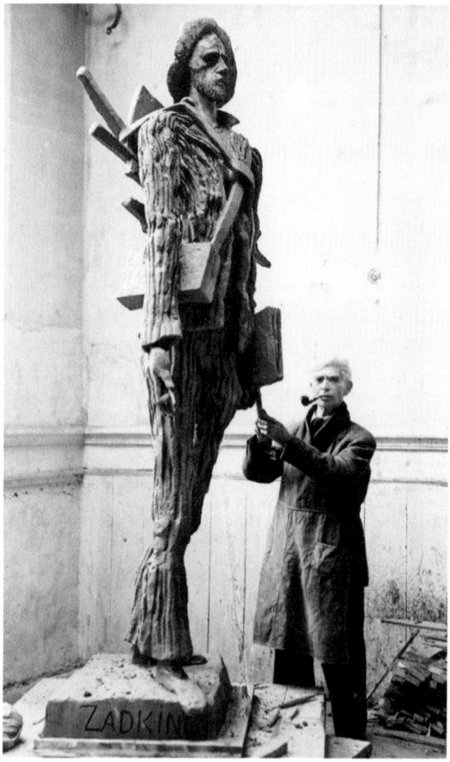

1

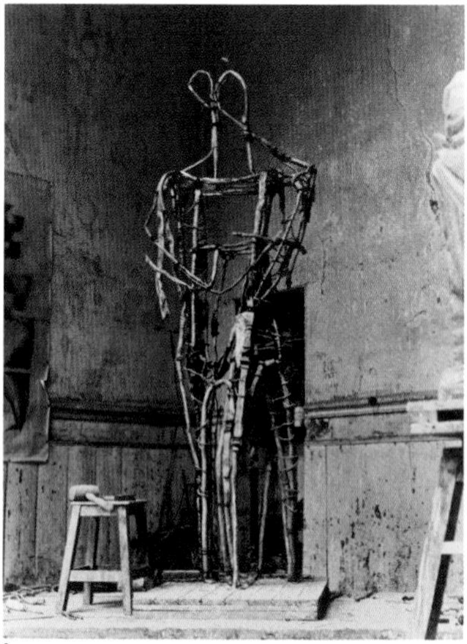

3

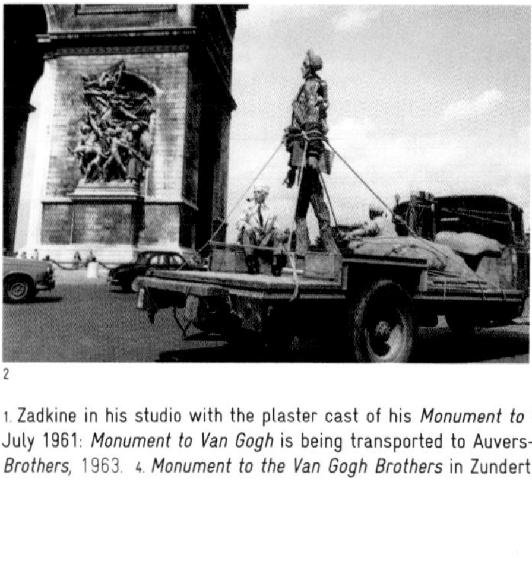

2

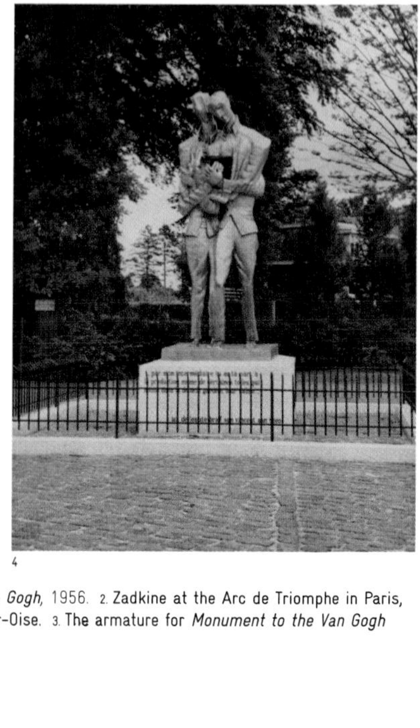

4

1. Zadkine in his studio with the plaster cast of his *Monument to Van Gogh,* 1956. 2. Zadkine at the Arc de Triomphe in Paris, July 1961: *Monument to Van Gogh* is being transported to Auvers-sur-Oise. 3. The armature for *Monument to the Van Gogh Brothers,* 1963. 4. *Monument to the Van Gogh Brothers* in Zundert

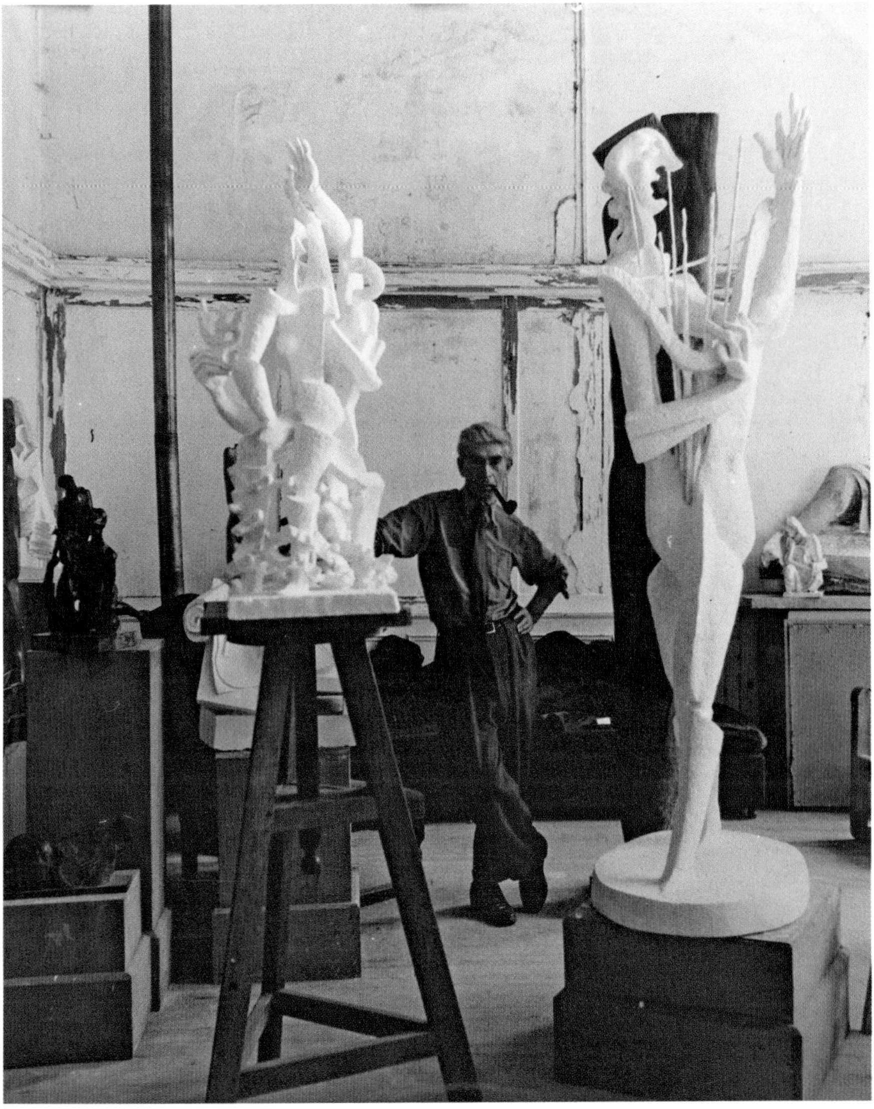

Zadkine in his Rue d'Assas studio, c. 1960

1959-1967

Major retrospectives mark this last period of Zadkine's life: at the Wallraf-Richartz museum in Cologne in 1961; the Tate Gallery in London in 1961; the Gemeentemuseun in Arnhem, Holland, in 1962; and the Kunsthaus in Zurich in 1965.

In addition two commissions, from the Bernard van Leer Foundation in Jerusalem (1960) and the Nederlandsche Bank in Amsterdam (1962), enable him to transform two earlier sculptures – *The Human Forest* and *La Demeure* (The Abode) – into works on a truly monumental scale.

In 1966 he has the pleasure of being commissioned by the city of Laval to carry through one of his 1939 projects for monuments to poets. The monument to Alfred Jarry is unveiled in the writer's hometown in 1968.

During the last two years of his life Zadkine moves into a new phase with a series of "Sculptures for Architecture", which he shows at the Lucie Weill gallery in June 1967 and intends to reproduce in very large-scale versions.

Already, in 1962, he has begun writing his memoirs, which are published in 1968 under the title *Le Maillet et le Ciseau, souvenirs de ma vie* (Hammer and Chisel: Remembering My Life).

In the autumn of 1967, after a last stay in Les Arques, he finishes the bust of his writer friend Claude Aveline on 8 November. For health reasons the opening of his exhibition of engravings at the French National Library is postponed from 17 to 28 November; on the 20th he has to be taken to the American hospital in Neuilly for surgery, but the operation comes too late to save him, and he dies on the morning of the 25th. His grave can be found in the Montparnasse cemetery.

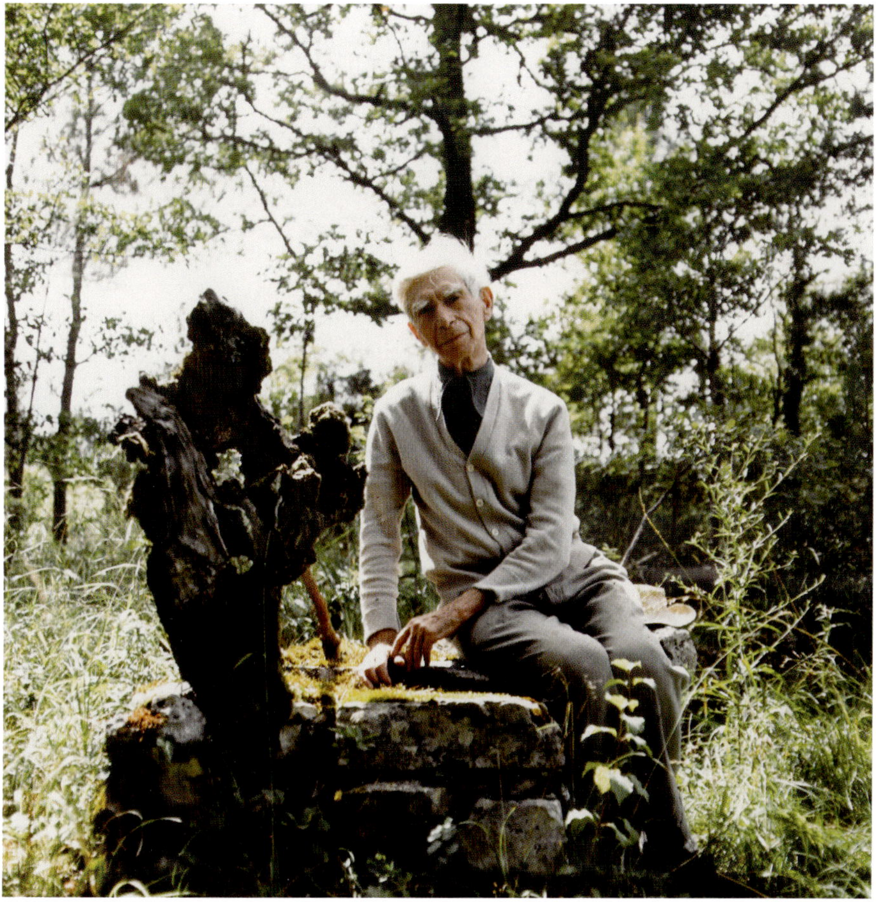

Zadkine posing with a tree trunk at Les Arques, c. 1965

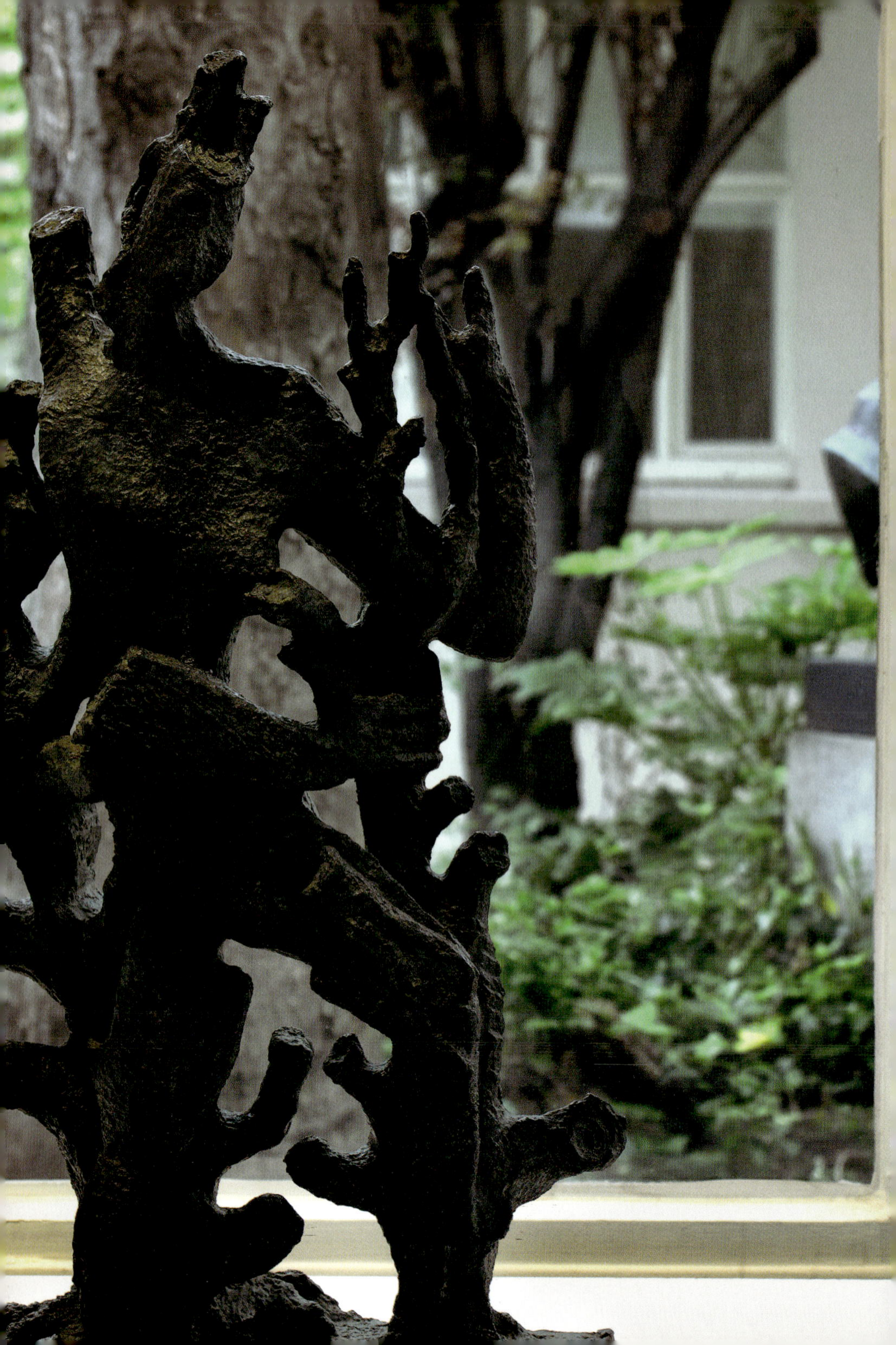

The Zadkine Museum

The collection provides a comprehensive survey of the development of Zadkine's oeuvre. Some seventy sculptures are on show in the five exhibition rooms and the garden.

Each of the rooms is chiefly devoted to one of the major periods of the sculptor's career.

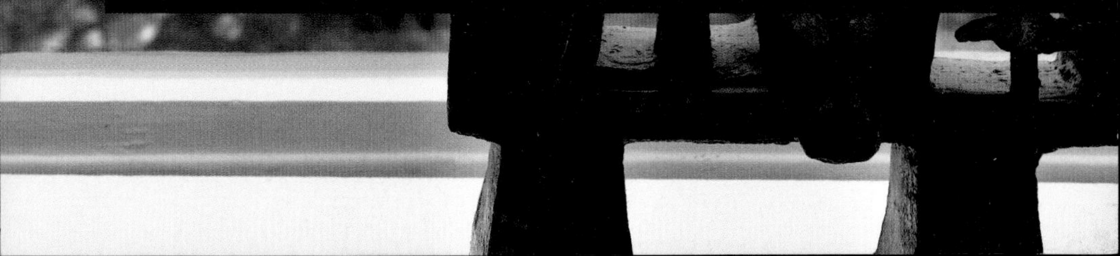

1913_1922

The early part of the oeuvre is divided up between Rooms 1 to 4 and is made up exclusively of works carved directly in stone or wood. In some cases Zadkine later decided to make bronze castings of statues like *Bust of a Girl* (c. 1913, Room 1), whose tapering hands, long neck and inclined head bespeak a slightly mannered approach. The ovoid head is reminiscent of certain works by Brancusi, who may have influenced Zadkine.
His first sculptures expressly made for casting in bronze only appeared in the early 1920s.

Room 1 is for the most part devoted to the works in stone and marble. Also on show are the earliest works in the museum's possession, among them the massive *Heroic Head*, probably carved in Russia in 1908. His *Mécislas Golberg* is a rare surviving example of the many portraits Zadkine produced until 1912, when he abandoned the genre as too

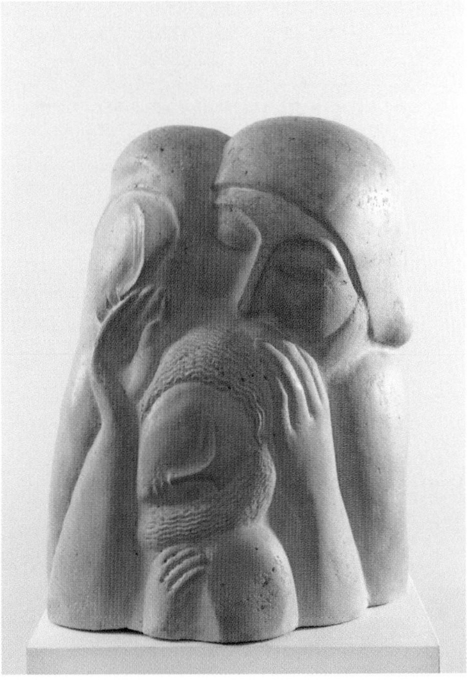

The Holy Family, cement, 1912–1913, 48 x 34 cm

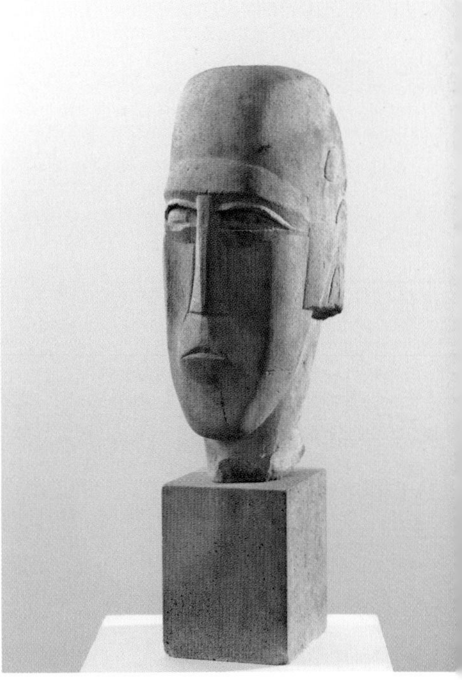

Head with Lead Eyes, stone, c. 1919, 50 x 23 x 23 cm

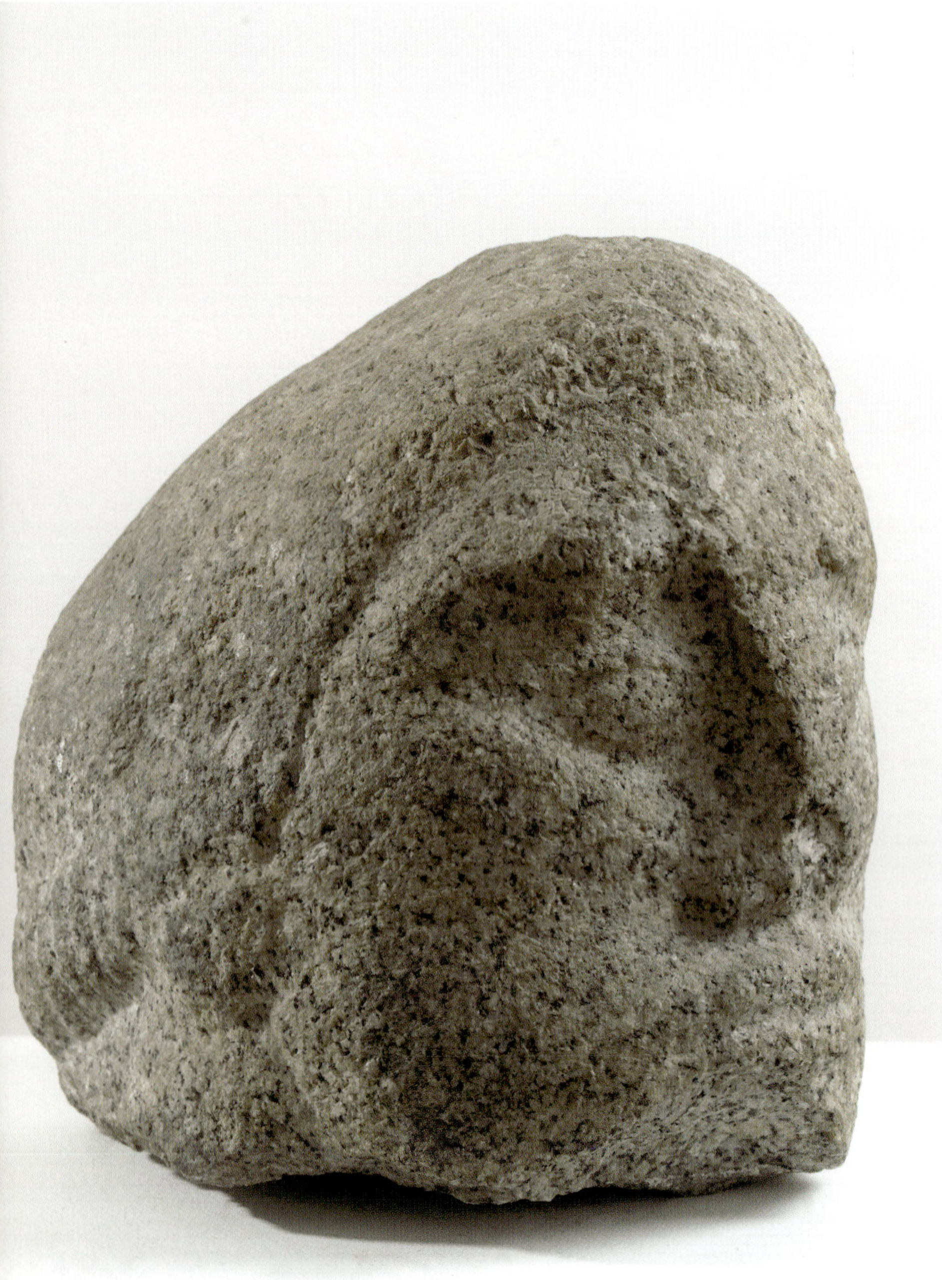

Heroic Head, granite, c. 1908,
27 x 29 x 28 cm

realistic – although he would return to it from time to time. Golberg (1868-1907) was a Polish anarchist philosopher who had moved to Paris in 1890, and there also exists a bust of him by Bourdelle. Cast in cement from an original in wood, *The Holy Family* (1912-13) is shot through with Symbolist inspiration.

The other sculptures in this room illustrate Zadkine's foray into Archaism. The stone *Head of a Man* (c. 1919) – the eyes were once filled with lead – displays the same elongated proportions to be found in the heads carved by Modigliani during the period when he was primarily a sculptor.

Motherhood belongs to a series of marbles dating from 1918–19 and characterised by the delicate, sensitive handling of a slightly raised surface that moved Maurice Raynal, author of the first monograph on Zadkine in 1921, to speak of "tender plasticity".

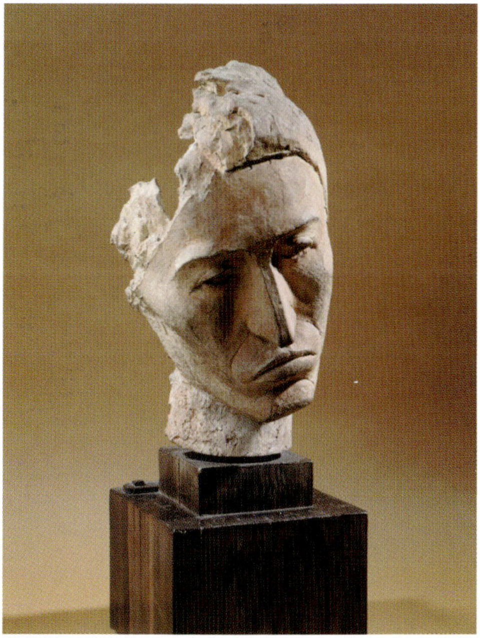

Mécislas Golberg, terracotta, 1912,
43 x 26 x 23 cm

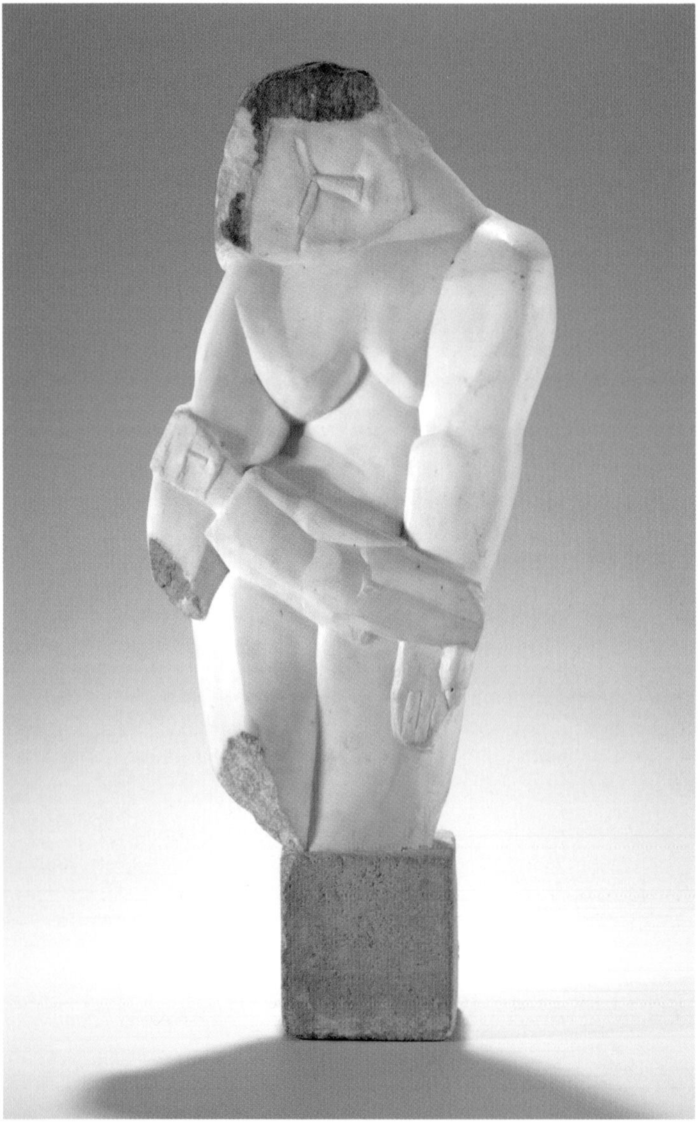

Motherhood, marble, c. 1919,
49 x 26 x 20 cm

Head of a Man in gilt wood (c. 1922) testifies to the level of subtlety the sculptor had already achieved by the early 1920s.

In **Room 3**, the stone pilasters with their figures carved in relief (c. 1922) once supported a mantelpiece.

Works in wood from different periods have been brought together in **Room 4**, among them four from Zadkine's initial phase: *The Grape Harvest* (1918) takes the form of a cylindrical frieze reminiscent of the paradisal worlds of Paul Gauguin and Georges Lacombe; *Water Bearer* (c. 1923), originally partly painted, is remarkable for its dynamism of line and the striking contrast between the narrowness of the waist and the forceful volume of the shoulders; once owned by the painter Jacqueline Marval, the large *Caryatid Venus* offers a powerfully robust, upright silhouette; and *Torso of an Ephebe* (c. 1922) harks back to pre-Classical Greek statuary.

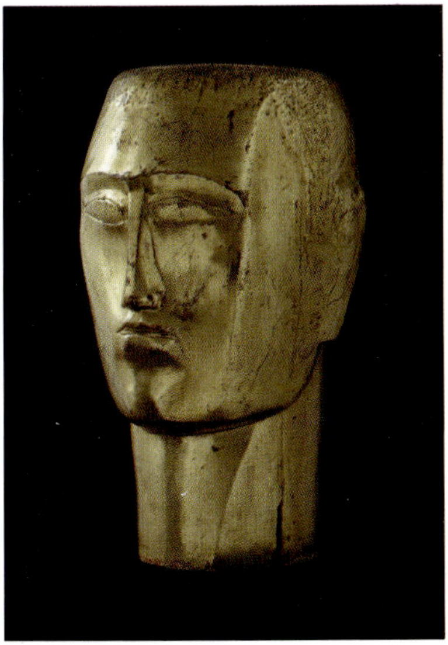

Head of a Man, wood and gold leaf, c. 1922,
39 x 22 x 25 cm

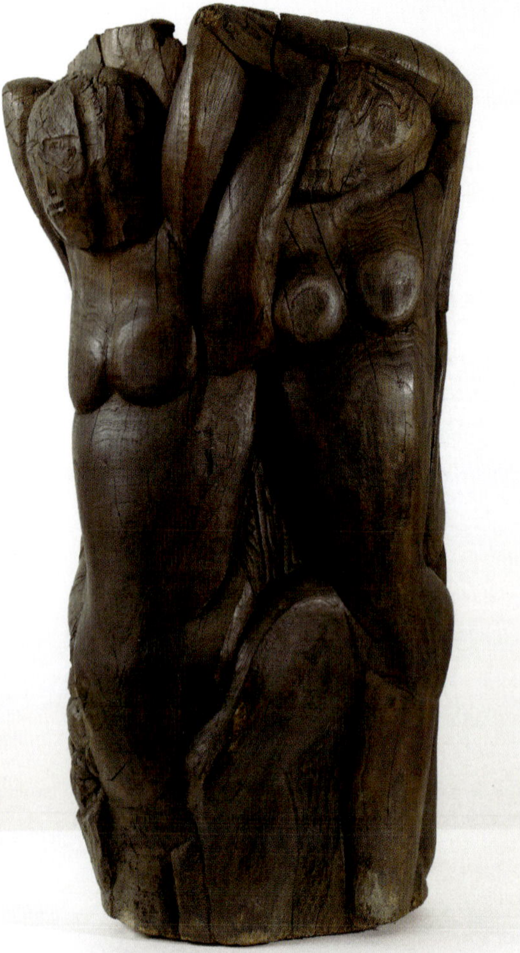

The Grape Harvest, elm, 1918,
97 x 55 x 40 cm

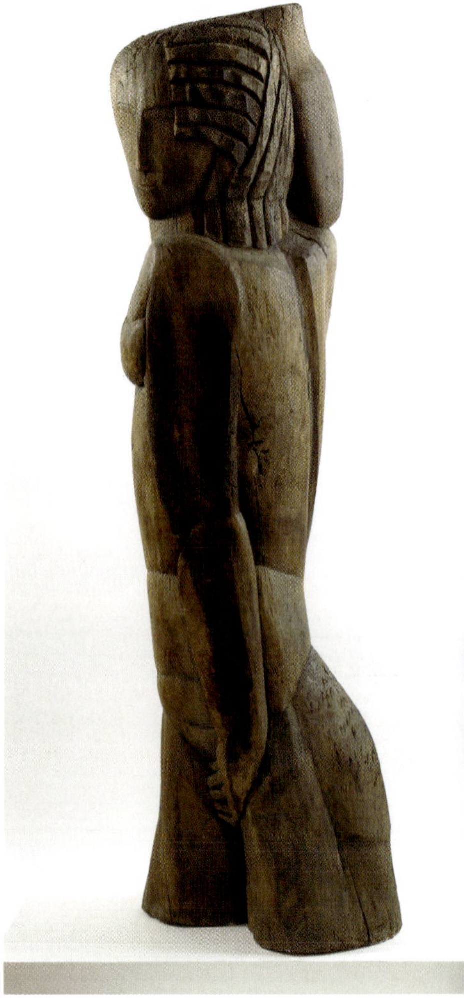

Water Bearer, walnut, c. 1923,
139 x 40 x 47 cm

Caryatid Venus, pear, 1919,
168 x 40 x 35 cm

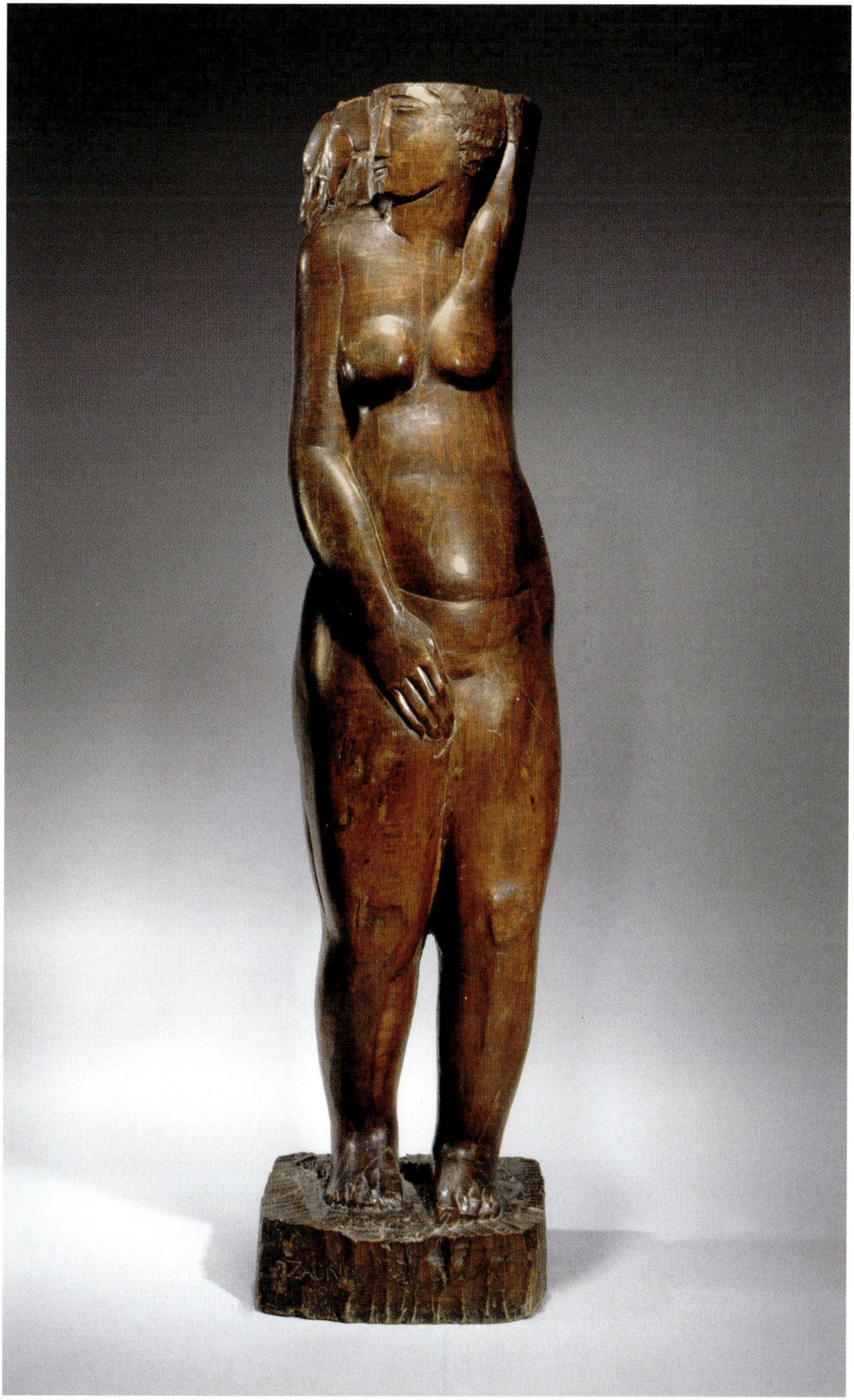

1922_1928

Often presented as one of the founders of Cubist sculpture, Zadkine in fact waited until the early 1920s before producing works in the spirit of what was a pre-war movement. **Room 2** is home to the pieces the most representative of his adoption of the new school's rigorous principles. The shift towards Cubism can be detected in the 1922 *Forms and Lights* – a polished bronze from a marble original – and the lava *Female Forms*.
In both he has preserved the massiveness of the block of stone, avoiding all protrusions by keeping the arms by the sides and the head laid flat on the shoulder. However, he has worked vigorously on the volumes within this compact mass, making systematic play with the contrast between concave and convex.
The most extreme expression of Zadkine's move into Cubism is to be found in the even more accentuated geometry of *Woman with a Fan*, of which the stone original was shown at the 1923 Salon d'Automne, and *The Accordionist* (c. 1924). The formal rigour of the two works is established by the presence of those archetypally Cubist accessories, the fan

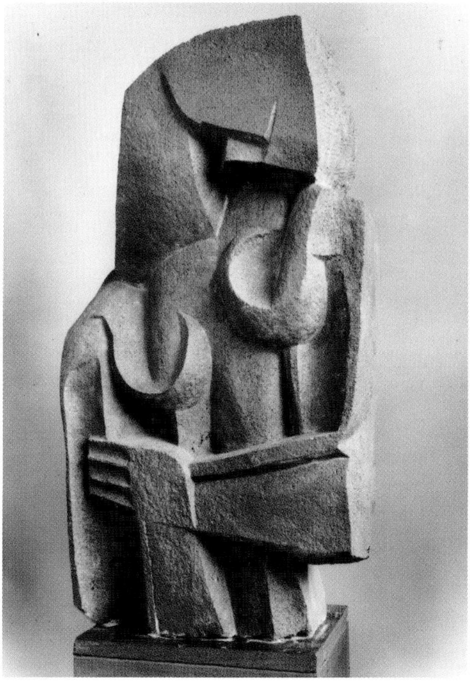

Female Forms, lava, c. 1922,
78 x 43 x 16 cm

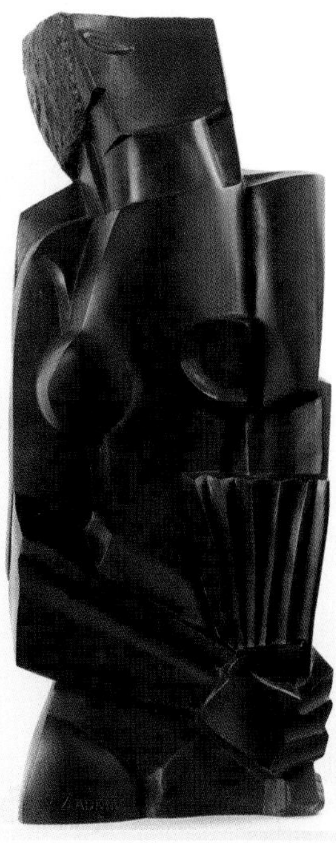

Woman with a Fan, bronze, 1923,
84 x 34 x 31 cm

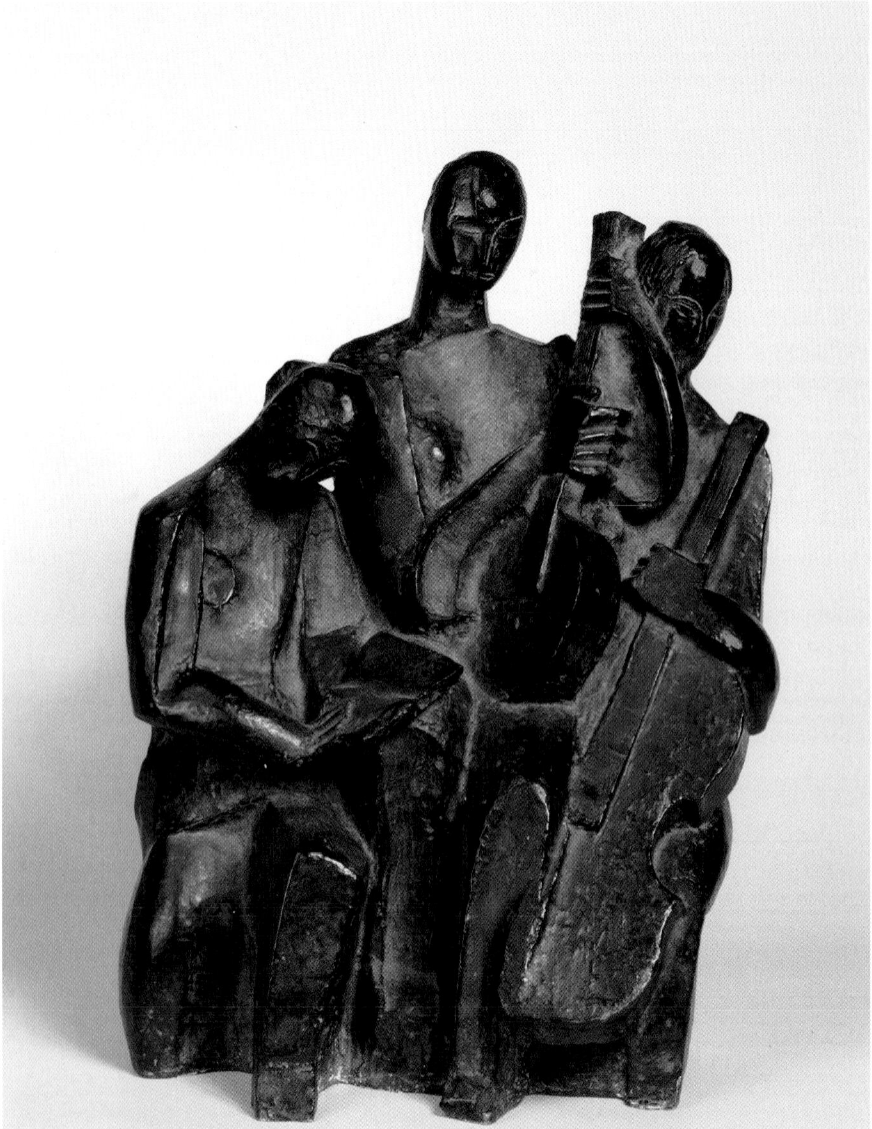

Concerto or *The Musicians*, bronze, 1927,
55 x 42 x 21 cm

and the accordion; and their geometry spills over into a human figure whose plasticity is subjected to the workings of an extremely precise visual mechanism.
For Zadkine, however, this formal austerity was no more than a phase, being too cramping for his lyrical propensity and need for emotional release. The demands of Cubism were too absolute for him to remain faithful to this extreme of rigid orthodoxy.

Concerto or *The Musicians* (1927) is among his first groups and reveals one of his most innovative contributions to the sculpture of his time. While most sculptors of his generation produced little apart from figures in isolation, there is, in Zadkine's work, a natural tendency for these figures to intermingle intimately, uniting to the point of fusion: not only among themselves, but also with musical instruments, architectural elements and,

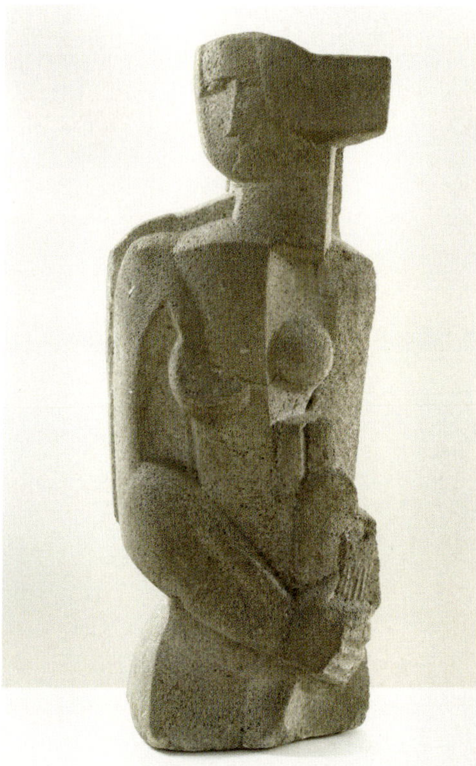

The Beautiful Servant, stone, c. 1926, 103 x 35 x 27 cm

in one large set of works, with plants. Thus do groups provide him with the potential for compositions based on multiple, complex harmonies of line.
Other works from this same period are to be found in Rooms 3 and 4 and in the veranda between Rooms 1 and 2.
With its more pronouncedly human side and greater fluidity of line, *The Beautiful Servant* (c. 1926, Room 3) marks the moment of Zadkine's break with Cubist inflexibility.

Also deserving of the visitor's attention are the lacquered wood *Torso of a Hermaphrodite* (1925–31, Room 4) and, in the veranda, the painted and gilded plaster of *The Golden Bird* (1924), the latter evocative of certain pieces by Brancusi. As much objet d'art as sculpture, this piece closely reflects the Art Deco aesthetic of its time.

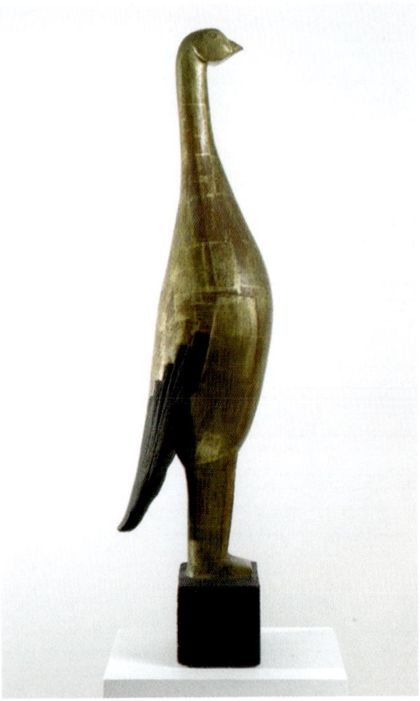

The Golden Bird, painted and gilded plaster, 1924, 86 x 21 x 26 cm

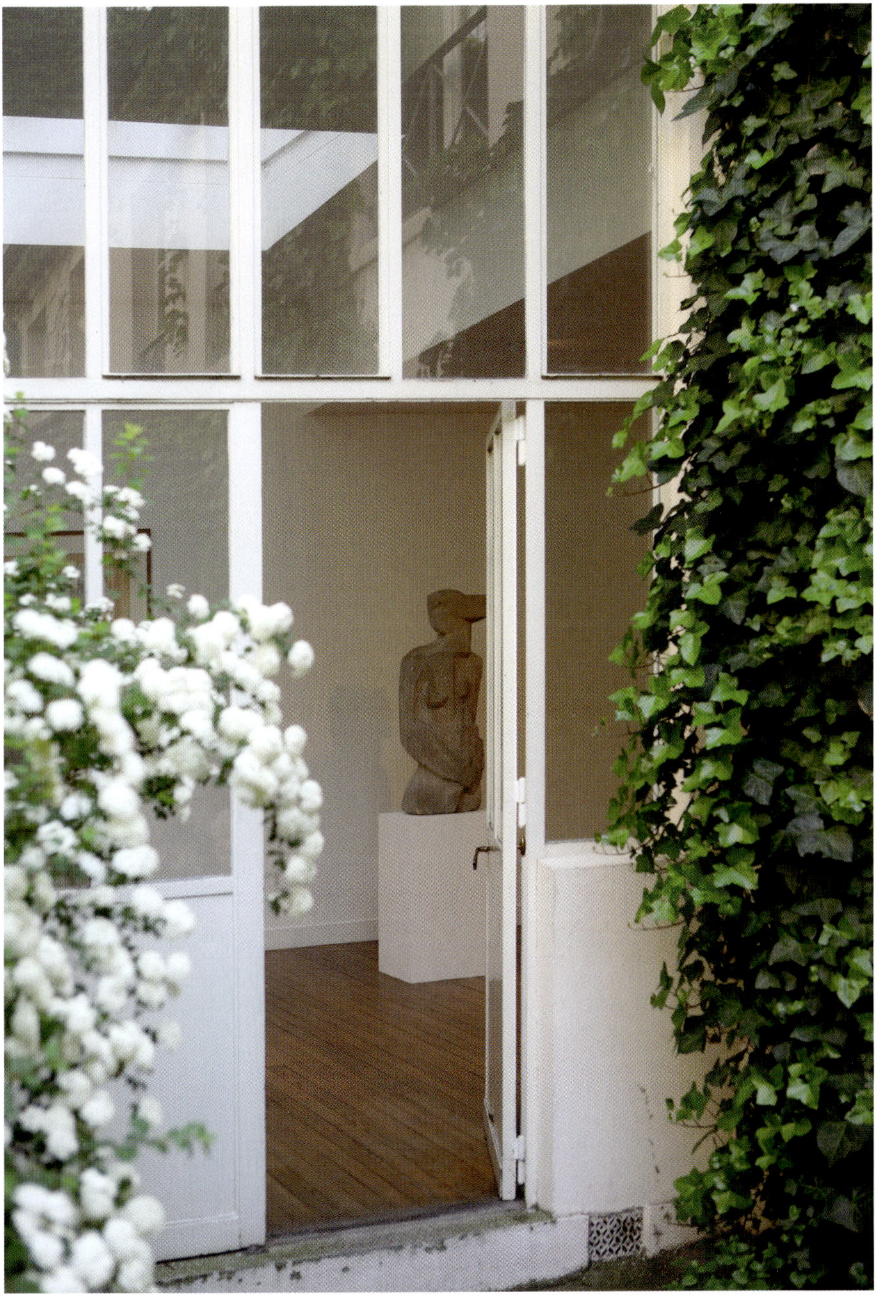

Room 3 of the museum seen from the garden

1929_1939

Room 3 shows Zadkine leaving behind the strict geometry of *Woman with a Fan* in quest of the easeful folds of Greco-Roman sculpture. At the same time he is breaking free of the compact-block straitjacket by reinterpreting Classical themes and injecting life into his sculptures with movement and gesture that generate harmonious voids and allow limbs to reach out freely into the surrounding space.
It was also at this time – although he would never totally abandon direct carving – that he began working more and more in plaster and clay, with a view to casting in bronze.
He nonetheless clung to the Cubist practices of jagged limbs, near-systematic inversion of concave and convex, and geometrisation of faces.
And by taking mythology as his wellspring he succeeded in clearly communicating the poetic and lyrical character of his work.

The evolution of the oeuvre towards greater humanism, fluidity and complexity found a perfect illustration in *The Maenads*, shown at the Salon d'Automne in 1929.
The forward rush of these three creatures seemingly fused together as one is splendidly captured in the controlled repetition of flowing lines. Seen in profile the work is suggestive of the breakdown of the phases of movement that was so dear to the Futurists.
In the garden another group of figures, *Birth of Venus* (1930), also dates from this period.
Expressions of the Cubist-inflected Neo-Classicism of Zadkine's 1930s are to be found in *Large Draped Figure* or *Melancholy* (c. 1929), of which an enlarged version is on show in the garden, *The Drawing Lesson* (c. 1936) and *The Messenger* (c. 1937). In this respect he is part of the nostalgic return to tradition that marked those years, although he never fell into the trap of a cold, excessively backward-looking art.

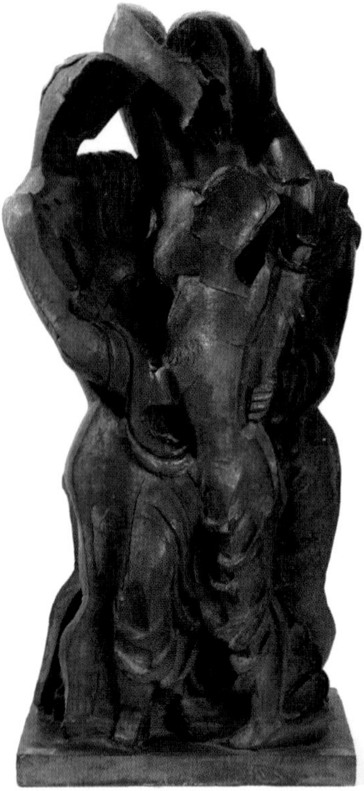

The Birth of Venus, bronze, 1930,
114 x 54 x 40 cm

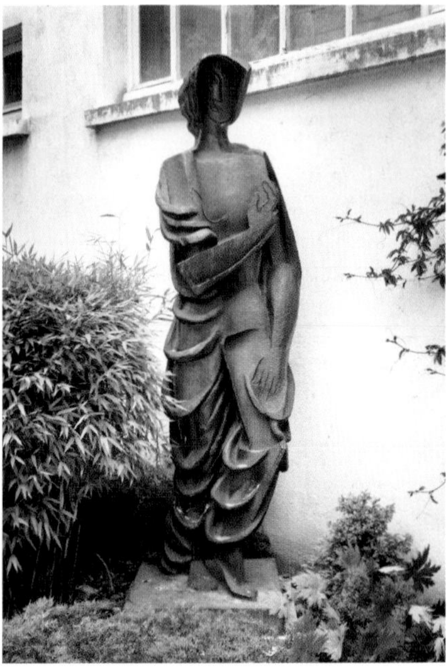

Large Draped Figure or *Melancholy*, bronze, 1929-1937,
192 x 58 x 51 cm

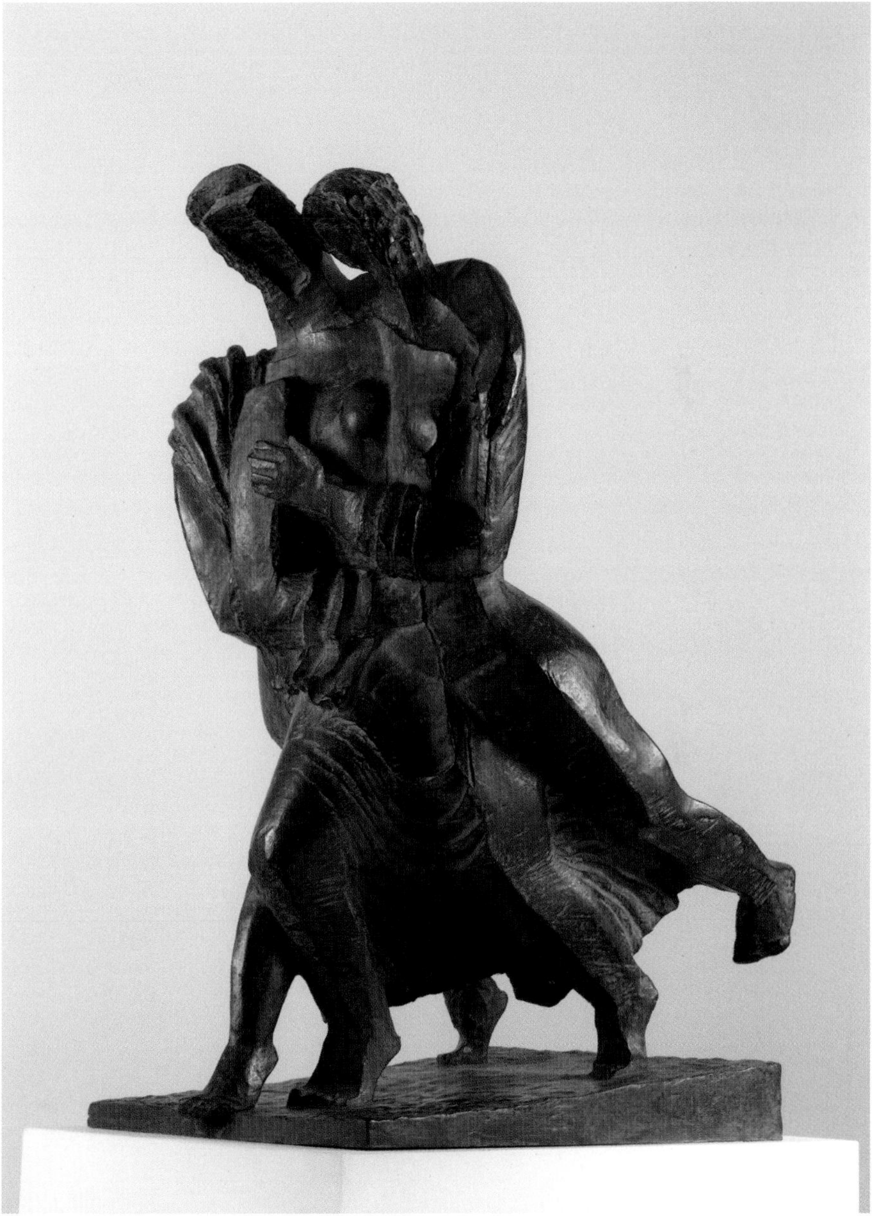

The Maenads, bronze, 1929,
76 x 35 x 52 cm

Room 4 contains four works that point up a fresh stage in Zadkine's development. These are the preliminary versions for monuments to the poets Alfred Jarry, Lautréamont, Guillaume Apollinaire and Arthur Rimbaud, as they were created in 1937–38 and shown at the Galerie Montaigne in 1939.

Enigmatic sculptures born out of deep poetic meditation, they offer hybrid beings rising up out of bases sliced into hollowed-out strips. Only Jarry is given any sign of light-hearted detail. A substantial part of the later oeuvre would have its source in these four singular works, of which their creator would write in his autobiography, "The works I consider as most important from this pre-1940 period are my four projects for monuments to the poets."

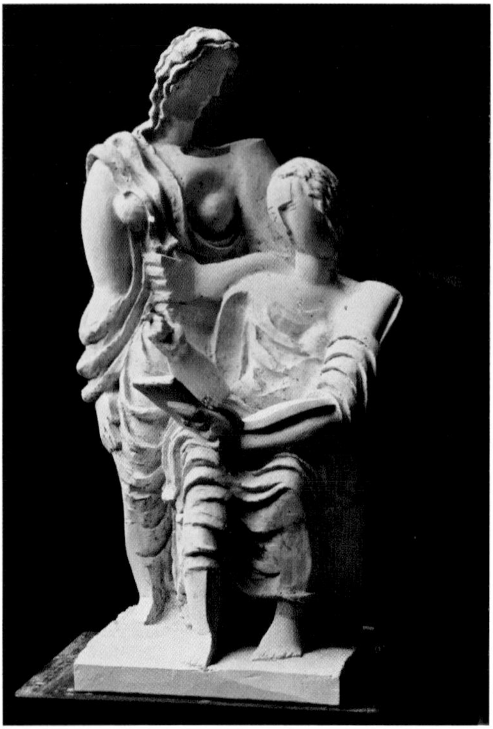

The Counsellor or ***The Drawing Class***, plaster, c. 1936, 66 x 34 x 28 cm

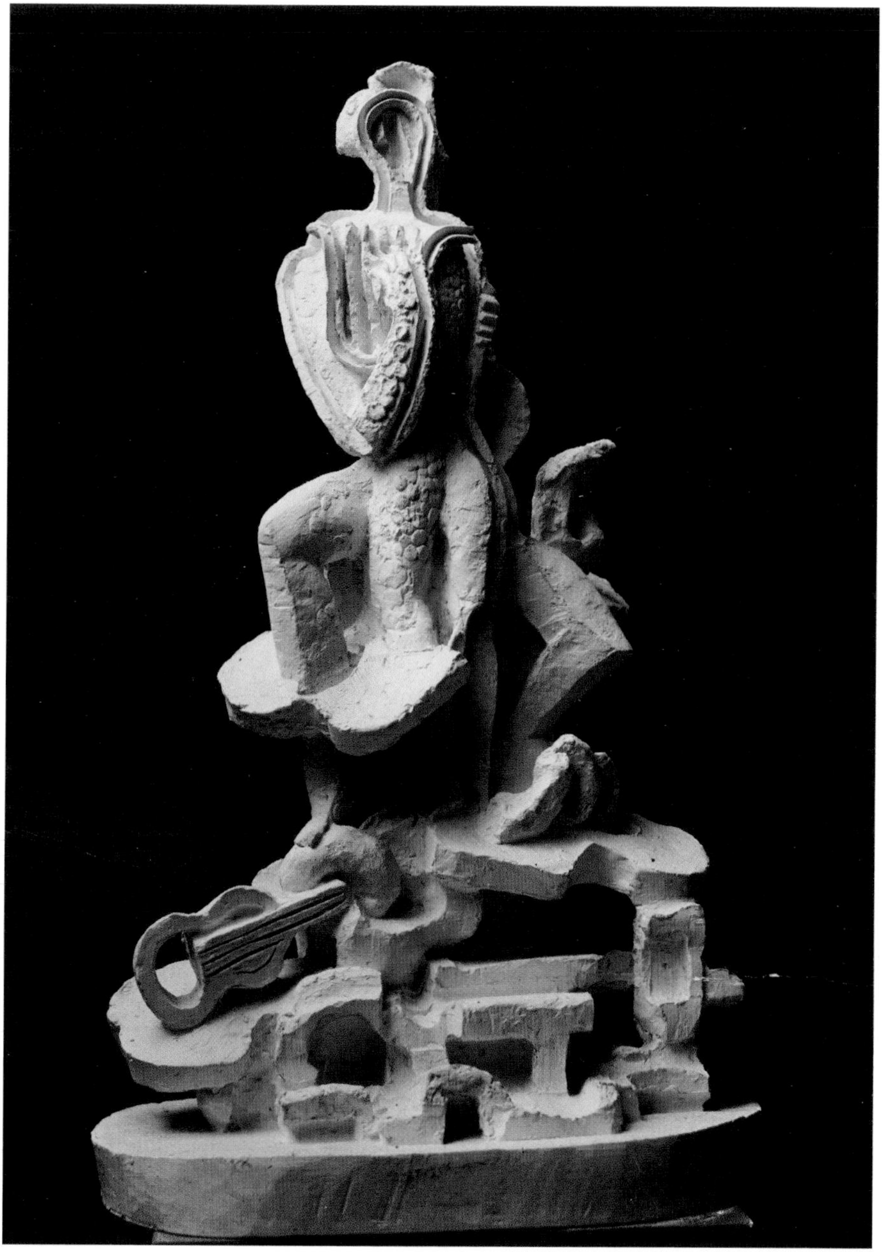

Rough of Monument to Arthur Rimbaud, plaster, c. 1938,
96 x 43 x 52 cm

1940_1967

The works from these years are on show in **Rooms 4 and 5**.
Zadkine's output during his American exile is represented by *Study for The Prisoner*, an expression of the anguish and despair then gripping the world and captured by the sculptor in a tightly closed three-sided figure. This model was used as the basis for a version almost two metres tall.

Obviously distressed by a life in exile that was so hostile to inspiration, Zadkine, on his return to Paris, was nonetheless able to pick up the creative threads and by 1946-47 his work was well under way again.

With their balanced combinations of solids and voids the complex new sculptures he now began producing were extensions of the poet monument projects of the late 1930s. Here he shows how a sculpture can be given an upthrust enabling its forms to emerge, gradually, from primal chaos. We also see him injecting new life into his group compositions, with the figures coming together, arms raised, in a shared upward impetus. The terracotta piece *The Labyrinth* (c. 1947) is typical of this conception of sculpture, as is *The Human Forest*, on display in the garden in an enlarged version of the 1947 original.

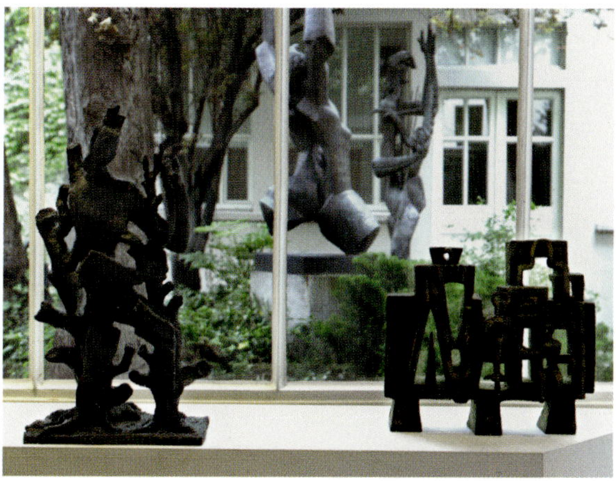

View of Room 5 of the Zadkine Museum. Foreground, left to right: ***Daphne*** (1958, bronze), ***The Portico*** (c. 1965, bronze). Behind, in the garden: ***Torso from To a Destroyed City*** (1951-1963, bronze), ***Orpheus*** (1956, bronze).

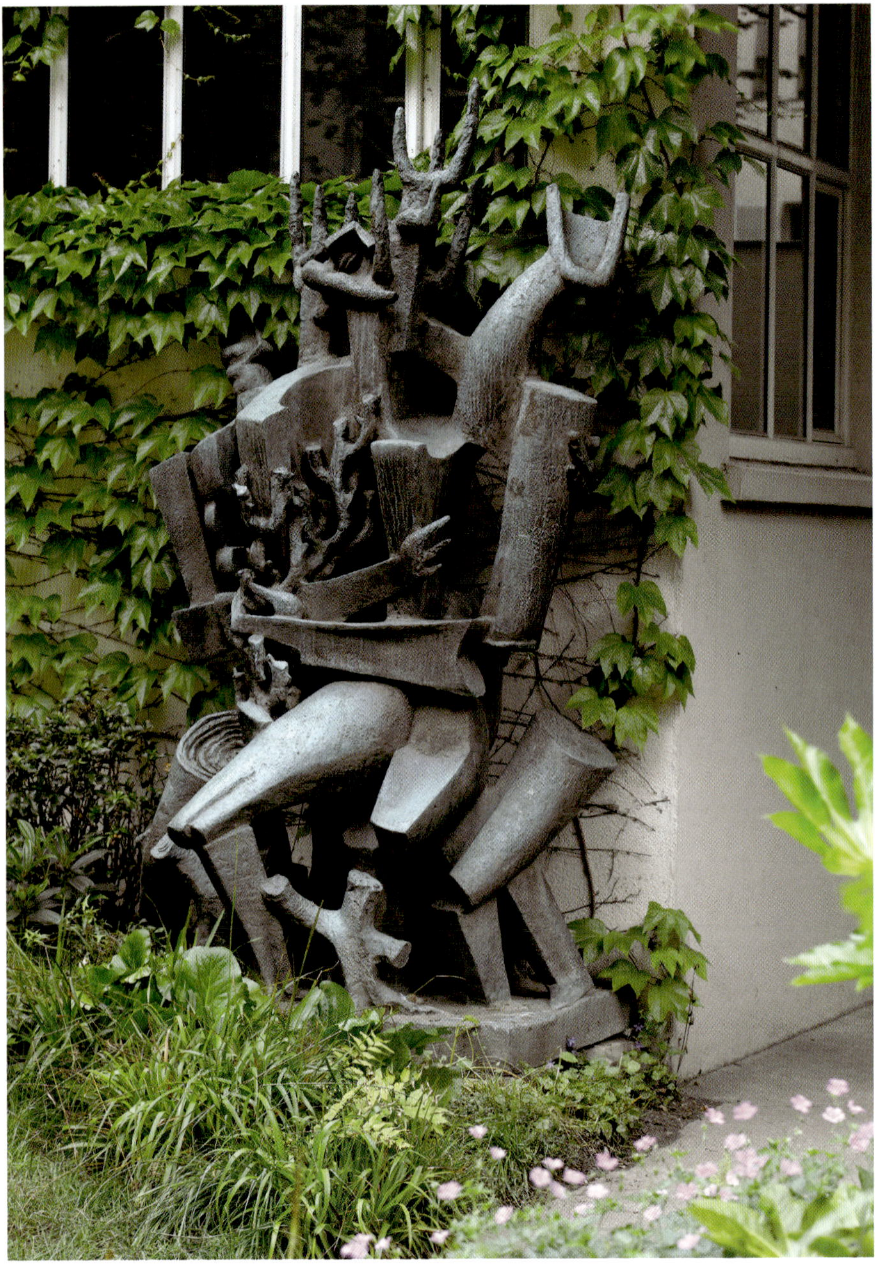

The Human Forest, bronze, 1957-1958,
240 x 125 x 98 cm

A new poetic vein springing from his intimate relationship with wood then made its appearance: that of a fusion between the human and the vegetal. *Sylva* (1951) in the garden, together with *Daphne* (1958) and *Girl in the Bloom of Youth* (1967) in Room 5 embody a meditation on an osmotic connection between two different natural states that can lead to an ideal harmony.
Vibrating in time with the strings of his lyre, the 1956 *Orpheus* in the garden can be taken as a manifesto, an assertion of the sculptor's fundamentally poetic and lyrical notion of what his art was all about.
It was during this period that Zadkine produced the most famous of all his works: *To a Destroyed City*, already described in the biography in the first part of this guide. A version with shortened legs is on show in the garden.
Another group of works, in Room 4, highlights the ongoing character of his work with wood, and with ebony in particular. Using this exceptionally hard material, whose colour and density fully justify the transposition to bronze, Zadkine carved a number of seamless,

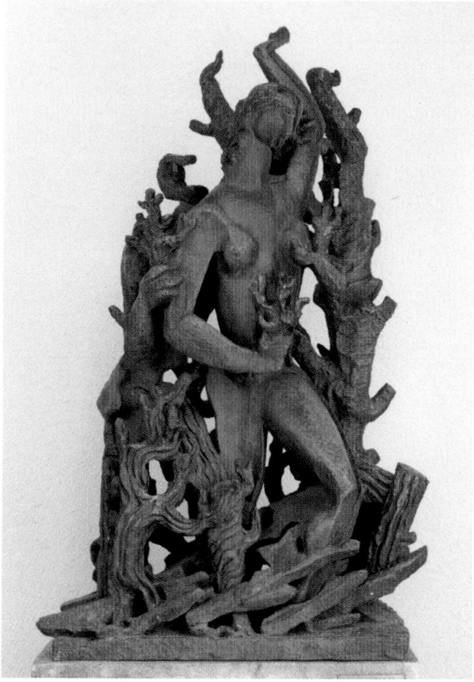

Sylva, bronze, 1951,
106 x 64 x 50 cm

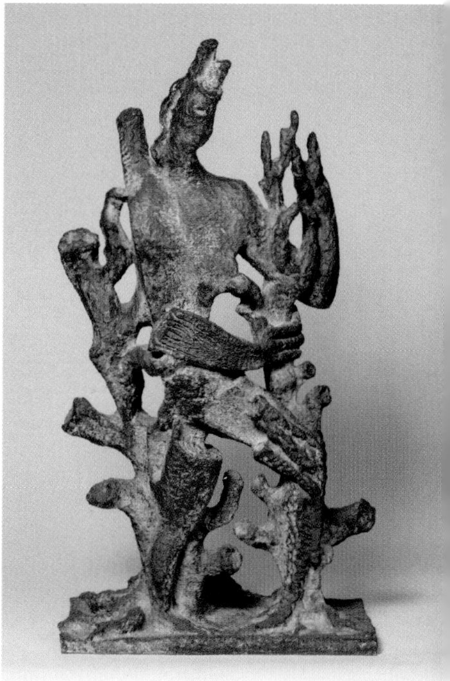

Daphne, bronze, 1958,
74 x 41 x 32 cm

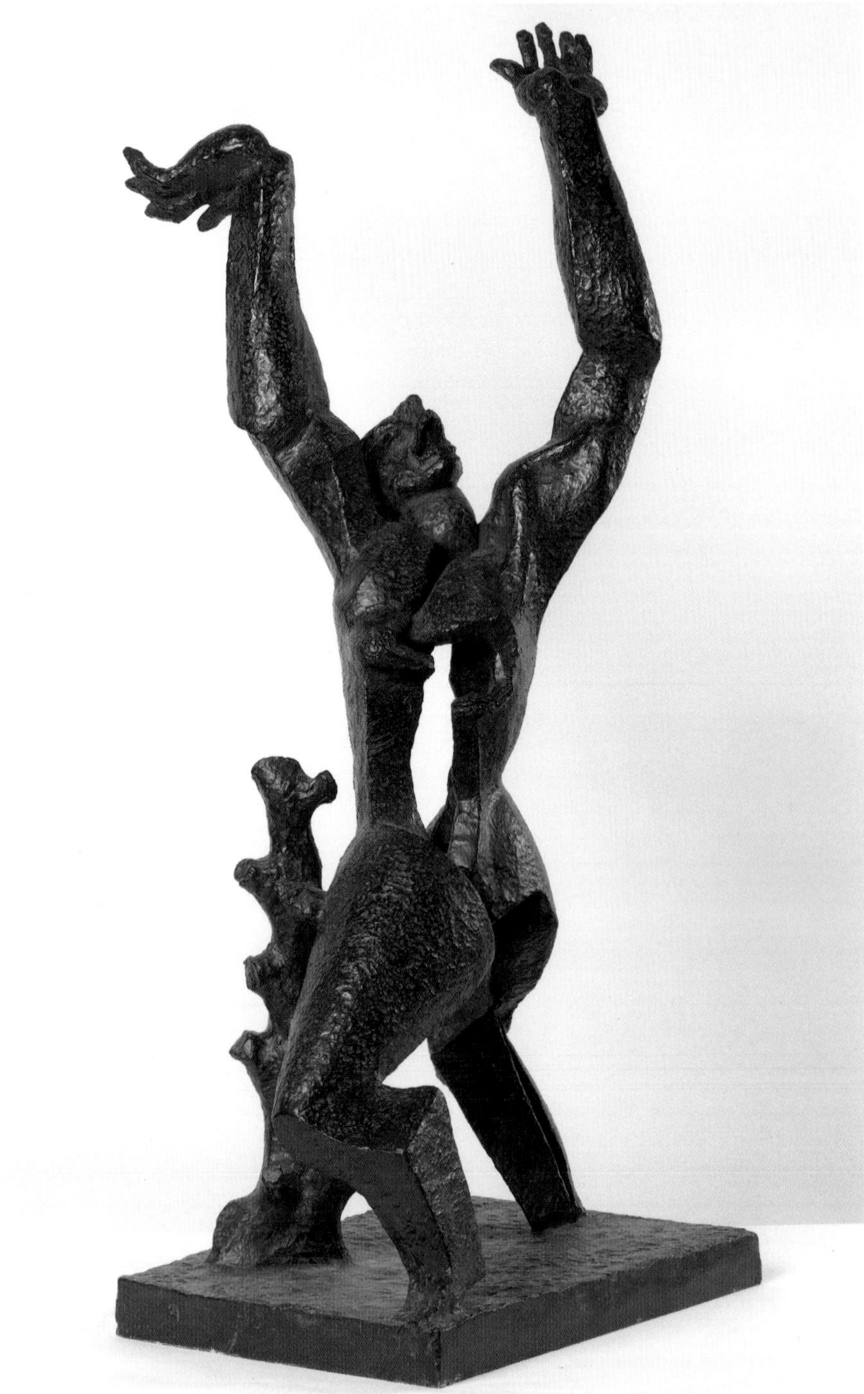

To a Destroyed City, bronze, 1947,
128 x 56 x 58 cm

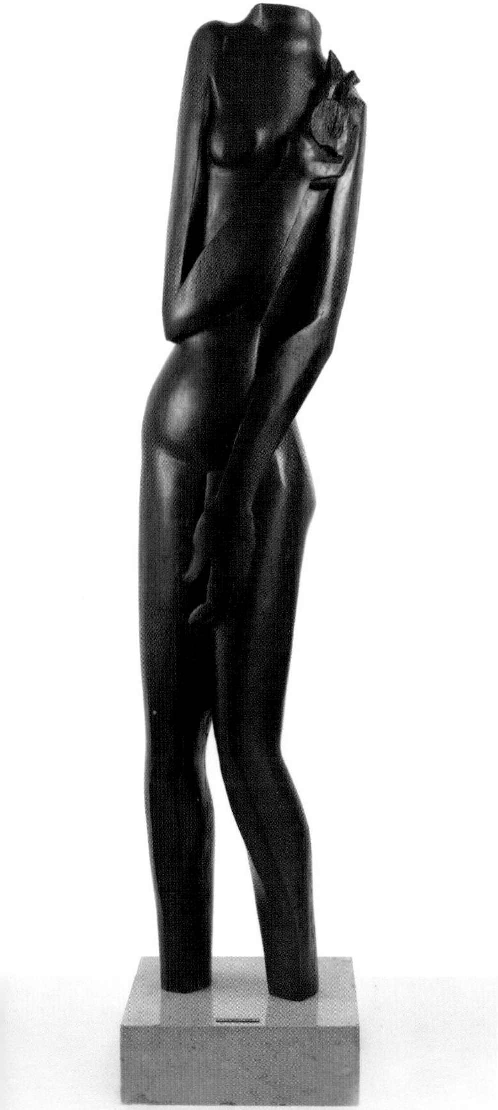

Demeter or ***Pomona***, ebony, c. 1958,
149 x 27 x 27 cm

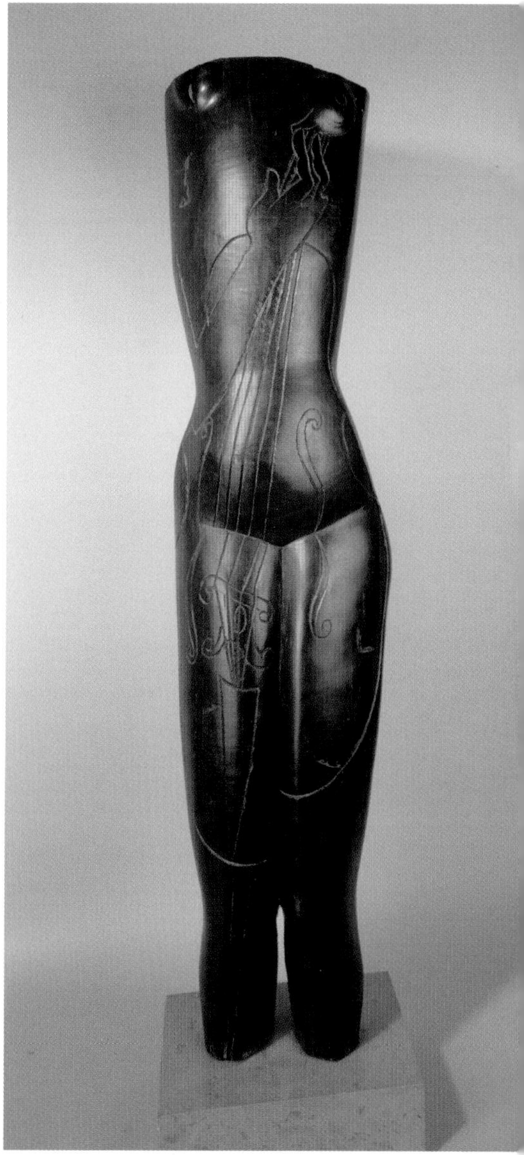

Cello Torso, ebony, c. 1956,
118 x 28 x 16 cm

pared-down figures completely at odds with the complexities and hollowings-out of the works in plaster and clay. *Pomona* (c. 1958) retains arms as true volumes while holding an apple which merges with one of its breasts. Zadkine had already taken simplification further with *Cello Torso* (c. 1956): the space between the legs is only (and very discreetly) indicated from the knees up and the arms are simply etched into the body.
Prometheus (1955–56) is one of the last large works in wood of his career.
The various monuments to Van Gogh he produced from 1956 onwards also played quite a part in his fame. In Room 5 are the preliminary sculptures for the monument to Vincent in Auvers-sur-Oise and the one to the Van Gogh brothers in Zundert.

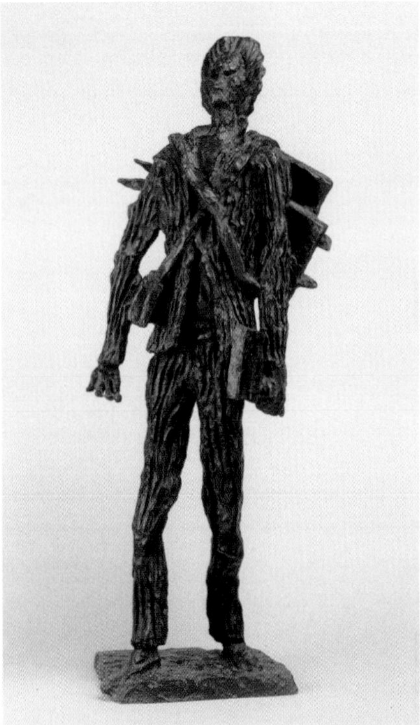

Rough of Monument to Van Gogh, bronze, 1956, 79 x 31 x 25 cm

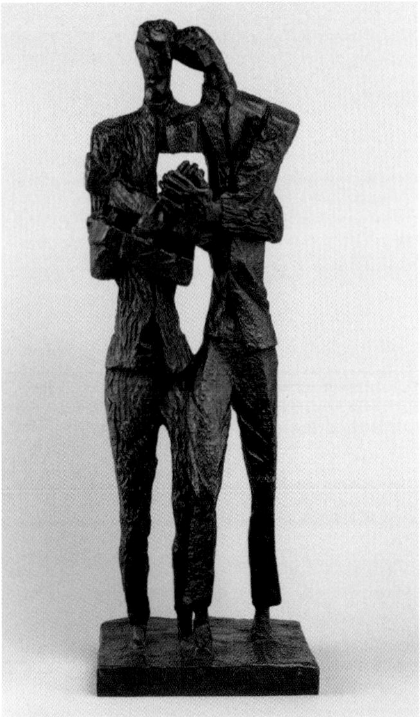

Rough of Monument to the Van Gogh Brothers, bronze, 1963, 79 x 28 x 23 cm

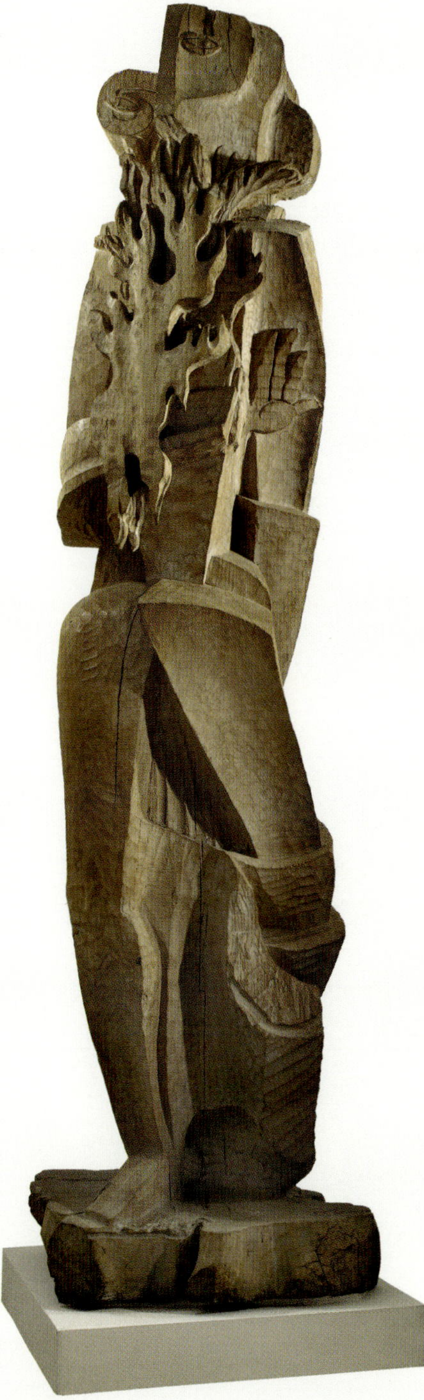

Prometheus, elm, 1955-1956,
300 x 69 x 98 cm

Most of the other pieces in this room point to the capacity for self-renewal Zadkine showed until the very end of his life. Whereas the human figure had been, until now, almost his sole subject of study, in the late works we see it all but disappear. Largely lost in the intertwinings of *The Abode* (1959), it can still be detected in *The Portico* (c. 1965), but has vanished from *Cruel Gate*, also of 1965. Zadkine exhibited these works in 1967 – the year of his death – under the umbrella title of *Sculptures for Architecture*, and contemporary photomontages show that he intended to enlarge them to monumental proportions as a challenge to the austerely rational architecture of the 1960s.
In the two 1967 plaster works in Room 4, we see sculpture itself become architecture, with a little staircase at the base of *Leaning Tower* inviting us to go inside, at least in our minds.

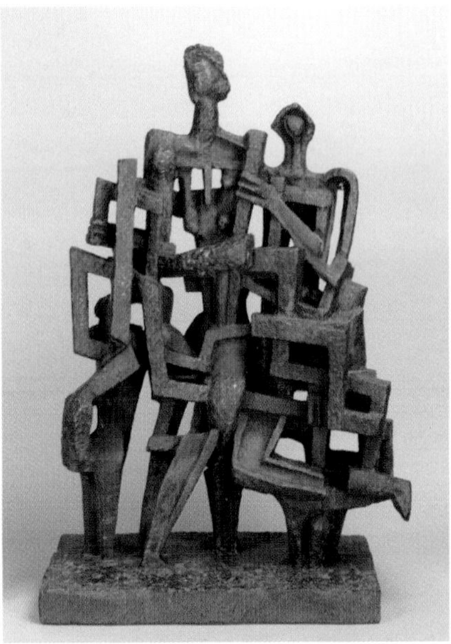

The Abode, bronze, 1963,
92 x 60 x 31 cm

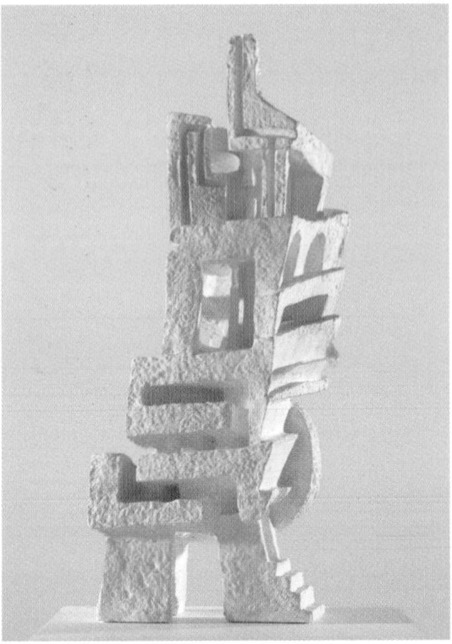

Leaning Tower, plaster, 1967,
53 x 23 x 17 cm

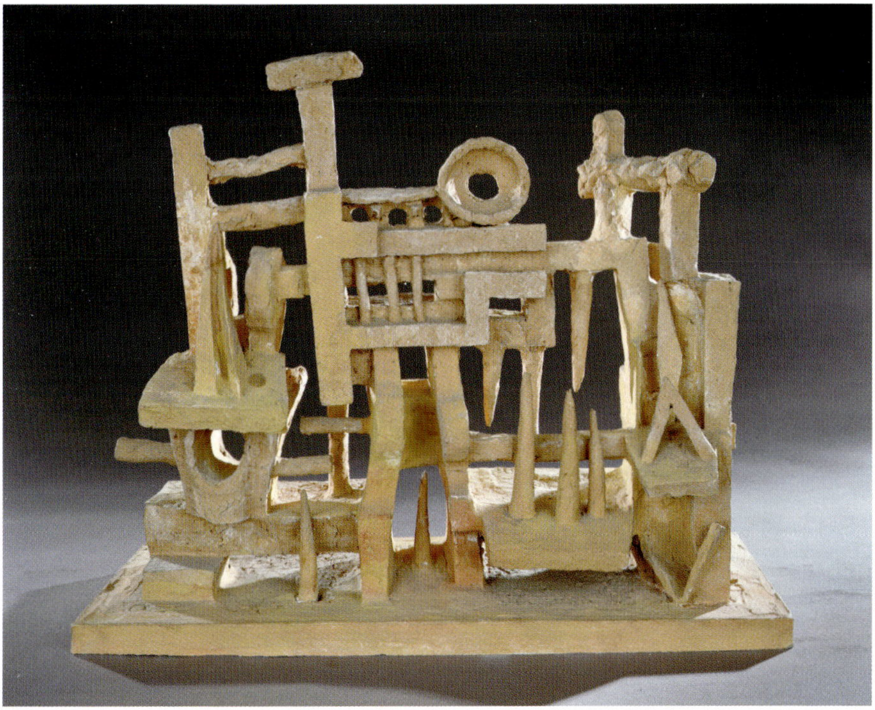

Cruel Gate, terracotta, 1965, 41 x 50 x 20 cm

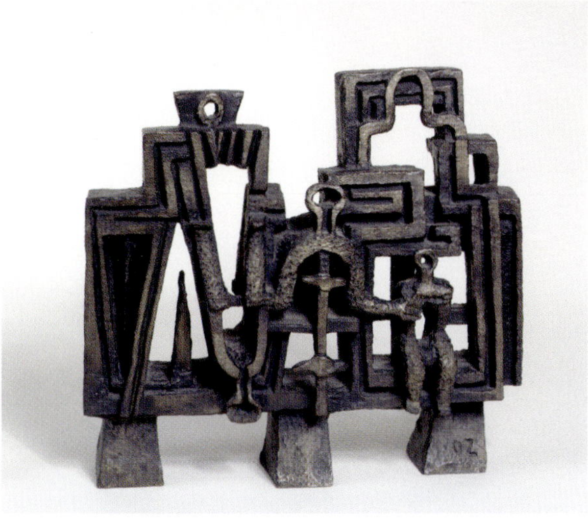

The Portico, bronze, c. 1965, 44 x 48 x 15 cm

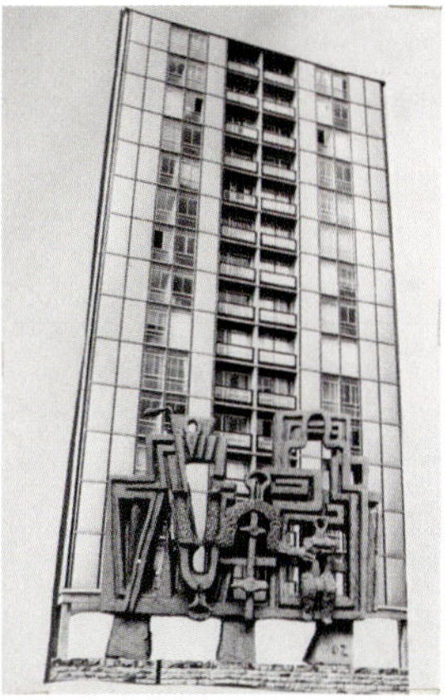

The Portico in front of a contemporary building (photomontage), c. 1965.

Zadkine in public places in Paris

Four sculptures are on show in public places in Paris. *The Messenger*, a bronze taken from a work in wood made for the tropical wood pavilion at the International Exposition in 1937, was unveiled on Place de Finlande, in the 7th arrondissement, in 1993. *The Poet* (1954), engraved with lines from Paul Eluard's poem "Freedom", was given a place in the Luxembourg Gardens in 1991. *Prometheus*, a bronze taken from a work in wood of 1955–56, was installed opposite the church of Saint-Germain-des-Prés in 1998. And *The Return of the Prodigal Son* (1964) has had a home outside City Hall in the 13th arrondissement since 1999.

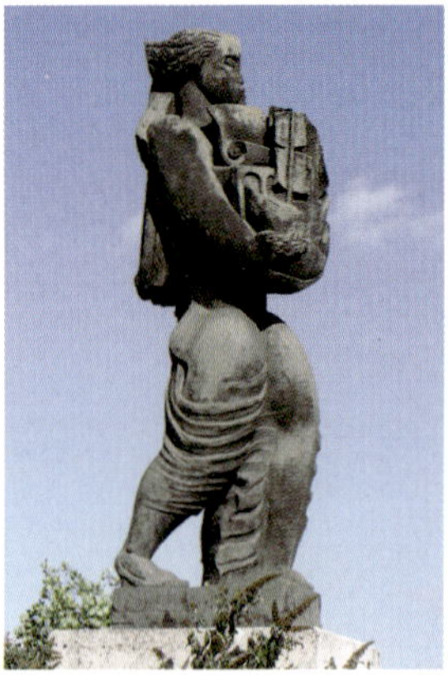

The Messenger, bronze, 1937, 340 x 100 x 75 cm

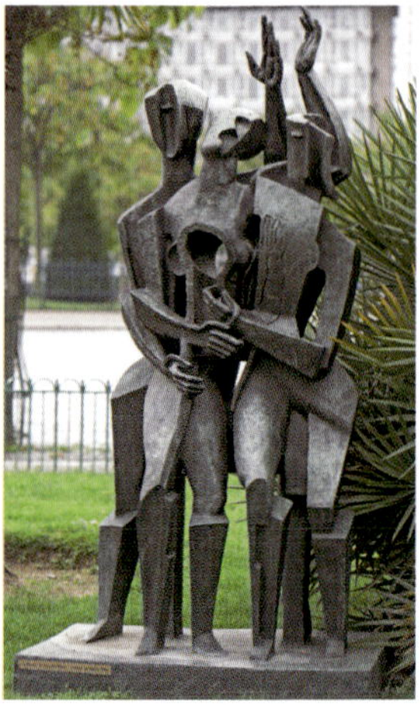

The Return of the Prodigal Son, bronze, 1964, 210 x 105 x 71 cm.

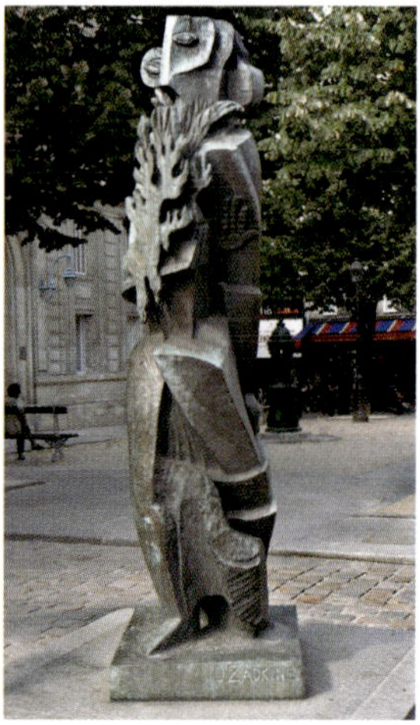

Prometheus, bronze, 1955-1956, 300 x 69 x 98 cm

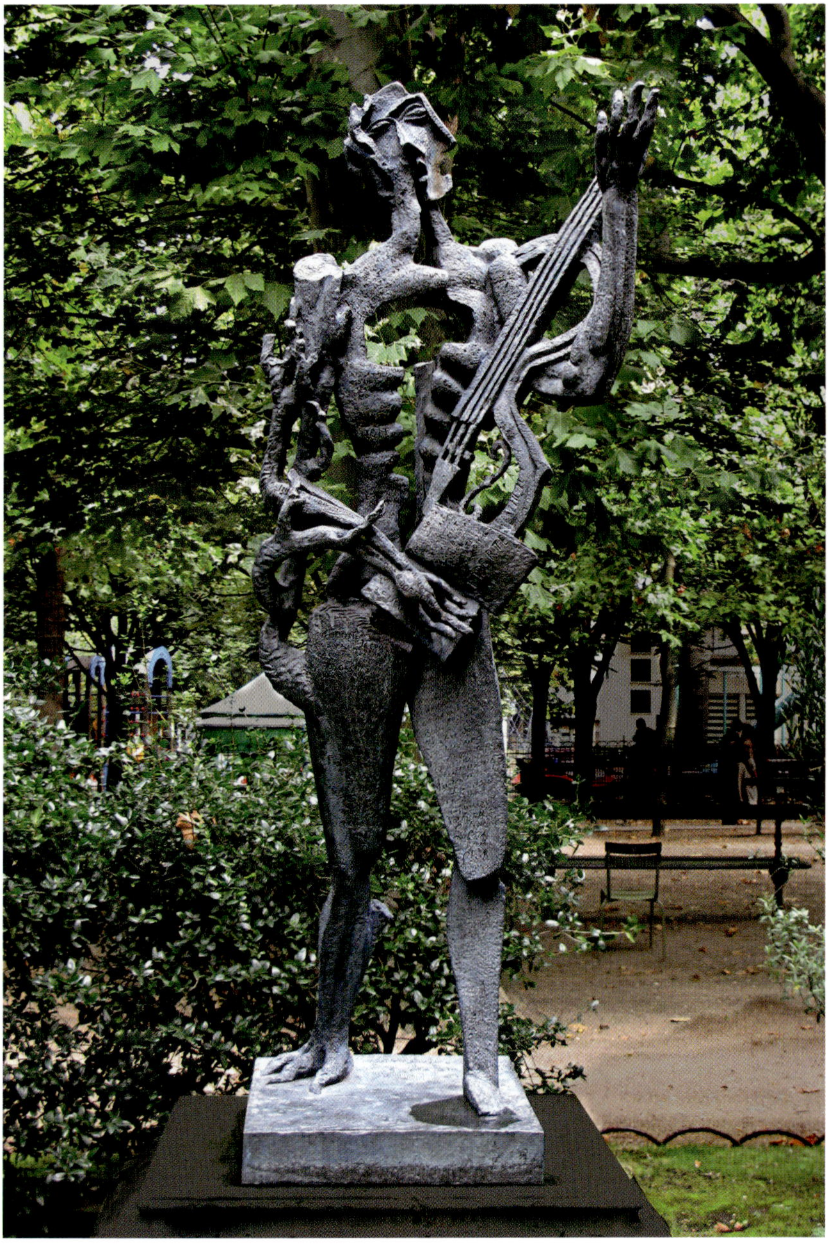

The Poet, bronze, 1954, 216 x 57 x 76 cm

The Zadkine Museum in Les Arques

In 1988 the Lot département established a Zadkine Museum in this handsome village where the artist bought a house in 1934. All the works presented are on deposit from the City of Paris, with the exception of the large *Christ* in the church, which belongs to the Musée National d'Art Moderne.

The visitor to the museum finds thirty sculptures representing the different periods of the artist's career. The most striking of them are the large works in wood: *Christ* (1938–40), *Pietà* (1955–57), *Daphne* (1939), the polychrome *Diana* in wood (1940) and the last, big *Orpheus* (1959–61).

Four large sculptures in bronze are also on show in the open air: *The Great Messenger* (1953), *Screaming Harlequin* (1956), *The Lotus Eaters* (1961–62) and *The Tree of the Graces* (1962–63).

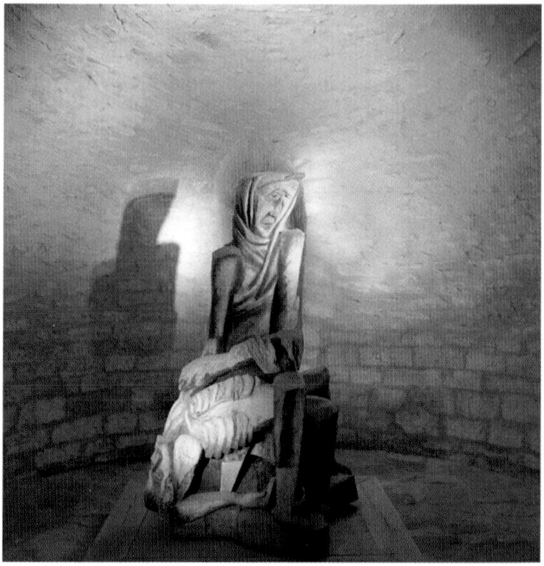

The crypt, Les Arques: ***Pietà***, 1955-1957, painted elm, 175 x 25 x 96 cm

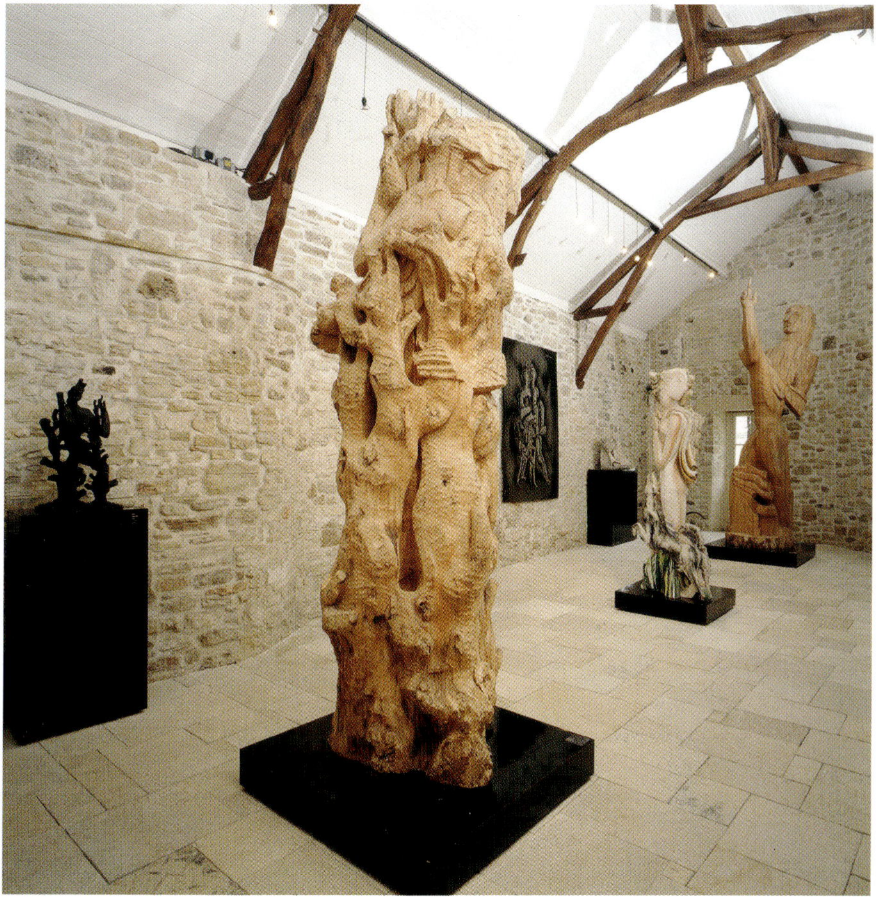

A room in the Zadkine Museum in Les Arques: ***Daphne***, c. 1939, elm, 291 x 120 x 70 cm. ***Diana***, 1940, almond, 198 x 80 x 57 cm. ***Orpheus***, 1959-1961, elm, 347 x 117 x 76 cm

Museum information

Musée Zadkine
100 bis, rue d'Assas
75006 Paris
Tél. 01 55 42 77 20
www.paris.fr
From Tuesday till Sunday from 10 am till 6 pm

Admission
During permanent collection:
free entrance
Temporary exhibitions:
with charge for admission

Public transport
Métro Notre-Dame-des-Champs, Vavin
RER B Port-Royal
Bus 38, 82, 83, 91

Photography credits

Clichés musée Zadkine/Parisienne de Photographie :
Bernard Citroën © succession Bernard Citroën : p. 18 (right);
Ladislas Czigany © succession Ladislas Czigany : p. 6, 19, 22 (top right);
Gene Fenn © succession Gene Fenn : p. 20 (left);
© Daniel Frasnay/AKG-Images : p. 22 (bottom left), 25;
David Nosek © agence VU : p. 4;
Marc Vaux © Centre Georges Pompidou-Bibliothèque Kandinsky :
p. 8, 11 (bottom), 15, 21, 22 (top left), 37 (left), 46, 47

© Conseil général du Lot/Nelly Blaya : p. 60, 61

© Didier Messina : p. 41

© Fr. Cochennec et E. Emo/musée Zadkine/Roger-Viollet : p. 29 (left), 30, 33, 34 (left), 37 (right), 39, 40, 44 (left), 45, 53 (left), 55, 56 (right);
Marc Dubroca/musée Zadkine/Roger-Viollet : p. 35, 57 (top);
Eric Emo/musée Zadkine/Roger-Viollet : 1re de couverture, 26-27, 29 (right), 34 (right), 49, 50, 58, 59;
E. Emo et S. Piera/musée Zadkine/Roger-Viollet : p. 52;
Philippe Joffre/musée Zadkine/Roger-Viollet : p. 32;
Philippe Ladet/musée Zadkine/Roger-Viollet : p. 53 (right);
Daniel Lifermann/musée Zadkine/Roger-Viollet : p. 31, 56 (left);
Jean-Marc Moser/musée Zadkine/ Roger-Viollet : p. 51 (left), 54;
musée Zadkine/ Roger-Viollet : p. 2, 11 (top), 12, 16, 18 (left), 20 (right), 22 (bottom right), 23, 44 (right), 51 (right), 57 (bottom right);
Patrick Pierrain/musée Zadkine/Roger-Viollet : p. 38, 57 (bottom left)

Design: Nicolas Hubert
Editorial: Stéphanie Méséguer
Translation: John Tittensor
Photoengraving: Fotimprim, Paris

28, rue Notre-Dame-des-Victoires
75002 Paris
www.parismusees
ISBN: 978-27596-0094-6
Copyright deposit: april 2009
Diffusion/Distribution: Actes Sud

Printed by Deckers Snoeck (Belgium) in march 2009.